ABYSS TO ZENITH: UP FROM INSANITY

ABYSS TO ZENITH: UP FROM INSANITY

One man's triumph over obsessive-compulsive disorder

Reagan Smith

Emerald Publishing

Printed in the United States of America

First Edition 1997
Paperback Edition 2002

Emerald Publishing
1632 Henderson St.
Harlingen, Texas 78550

Library of Congress Catalog Card Number 97-90475
ISBN 0-9658288-1-6

Cover art by B.J. Hammans

This book is dedicated

To my Lord and Savior Jesus Christ,
the Captain of my ship,
the Lord of my life.

To my wonderful wife Marsha, who has
always stood by my side.

To my mother and father, Jippy and M.C.,
the best parents a son could have.

To my four children--Brian, Paul, Julie,
and Melissa--the pride of my life.

To my sister Sheila, who has always been
an inspiration.

To Robert O. Collier, M.D.,
a skillful and caring physician
and friend.

ACKNOWLEDGMENTS

One of the most valuable gifts that the Good Lord has given me is the ability to surround myself with people who are wiser and more talented than I am. Three such individuals are my wife Marsha, my sister Sheila McCartor, and my friend Ouida Yeats.

The idea to write a book about my struggles with OCD originated with my wife Marsha. She helped and encouraged me during this entire project, and she worked tirelessly with me during the writing and rewriting of the manuscript.

I am grateful to my sister Sheila for her input in the writing and editing of several of the early chapters. Her assistance and support were very valuable and much appreciated.

This book would not have been possible without the talents and abilities of my dear friend and editor Ouida Yeats, who worked closely with me through several edits and all the way through to the final manuscript.

Always, I thank the Good Lord for giving me the right words and the strength to take this project to completion.

CONTENTS

FOREWORD

More than five million Americans, 2% of the population, suffer from obsessive-compulsive disorder (OCD), according to the Obsessive-Compulsive Foundation headquartered in Milford, Connecticut. This disease has been called the "secret" mental illness.

The billionaire Howard Hughes (1905-1976) and the Protestant reformer Martin Luther (1483-1546) suffered from this ailment. Samuel Johnson (1709-1784), one of the most noted men of his age--playwright, poet, biographer, lexicographer and scholar, endured some version of this disorder.

OCD is a strange, fascinating (except to the victim), often destructive, and sometimes debilitating illness which is marked by the intrusion of insistent, repetitious, and unwanted thoughts. It is characterized by impulses to perform repeatedly certain acts or to carry out certain rituals.

This book is a personal account of one who endured the ravages of obsessive-compulsive disorder (and related disorders, namely: panic attacks, phobias, and depression) and who rose victoriously.

This is a book about combating and conquering mental illness. For 20 years, beginning as a child, I kept my illness a secret, terrified that revealing it would mean commitment to an insane asylum. Only after years of torment (at age 26) did I in total desperation seek help. But even with psychiatric assistance, I fought a battle that raged on for an additional 12 years.

By writing this book, I wish to offer encouragement to those individuals who are still suffering in silence. It is my hope that these individuals, their families, and their friends come to realize that persons with these ailments can lead happy, successful, and productive lives.

The Author
August 2002

PREFACE

This is a story about victory, not defeat. These episodes describe my personal struggle against an unseen enemy within, an enemy so ruthless that it almost destroyed my life. But by the grace of God and with the support of a loving, caring wife, the enemy is defeated. Life triumphs!

The reader should understand that mental illness is often not a continuous affliction. A person can be mentally ill for a time and then go into a remission that may last months or even years. During this period the individual may behave quite normally. Then, for no apparent reason, he/she can be plunged back into mental illness for an indefinite period.

For many years, I considered myself two separate beings. One *me* could be almost normal in thinking and behavior. This *me* was happy, ambitious, and enthusiastic most of the time. I liked this *me*!

The second *me* seemed almost another person. *He* thought thoughts that I did not want to think. *He* behaved in ways I did not want to behave. This *me* was a master at obliterating plans and dreams, a master at causing dreadful unhappiness. I hated this *me*! *He* was my enemy! This enemy controlled and dominated a vast portion of my life for over thirty years.

* * *

Once I had aspirations of becoming a medical doctor.

My illness dramatically changed the course of my life in every respect.

PREFACE

After graduation with a degree in biology from the University of North Texas, I applied to and was accepted by the University of Houston College of Optometry. This application and acceptance came after my dreams of becoming a physician had been crushed.

Then OCD changed my plans again, and my career goals took yet another direction. After several years of endless turmoil, constant struggle, and personal insecurity – years of searching for a way to use my education and feel a useful member of society – I decided to try my hand at teaching. Little did I know that this seeming compromise would become a fulfillment of many of my needs and aspirations.

I have been a classroom biology teacher for 23 years.

Teaching has been an enormously fulfilling and richly rewarding career for me since I conquered mental illness seventeen years ago.

Reagan Smith
Harlingen, Texas
August 2002

1 CHILDHOOD

At the age of five, I began worrying about catching some dread illness. I recall that my family and I went to visit some neighbors. The two neighbor kids were playing with their older cousin who had developed a case of ringworm on her head. I was told that she had had to have some of her head shaved for the ringworm to be treated effectively. This information hit me hard, and I became concerned that I would catch that awful disease. Having one's head shaved, I imagined, would be the worst thing that could happen to a kid. I was told that the cousin had caught the infection from a cat and that it could be spread from one person to another.

Our visit with the neighbors lasted several hours, and during the entire evening, I would not go near the cousin. I thought that just getting near the infected person might somehow cause that hideous disease to leap through the air onto me. That thought made me want to flee from this "diseased individual."

Upon arriving back home, I immediately went to the bathroom and washed my hands several times. I did not feel comfortable near a cat for a long time. I was sure that I was going to catch ringworm and that my head would have to be shaved!

Even at the tender age of five, my mind was beginning to behave abnormally. This was not a case of a small child's fearing something for a short time and promptly forgetting it. I thought about ringworm very often for many months.

A year or so later at school, I noticed on my arm a circular red mark about an inch and a half in diameter. I was horrified! I had caught the disease. I was going to have to have my head shaved. In misery I rode home on the school bus thinking of all the terrible things that would probably happen to me. At home, I showed my arm to my mother, and surprisingly, she did not seem at all alarmed. She simply said, "Reagan, did someone bite you at school today?"

Then I remembered. At recess that morning on the playground, I had gotten into a wrestling match with another boy, and he had bitten me on the arm. Was I relieved! The red ring had been caused by the boy's teeth. I would not have to have my head shaved after all.

I first learned of germs about the age of seven. I found out that they were little critters too small to be seen and that they could make me sick. I became obsessed with the idea that I was going to get some bad germs in my mouth and that they were going to cause me to contract a terrible disease. I decided that the only way I could protect myself was to spit them out of my mouth. So I began to spit and spit and spit. My spitting increased each day, and I did not know if I could spit enough to save myself from these creatures that were out to get me. Eventually, my mother noticed my frequent trips to the bathroom to spit, and she questioned it. I told her that I feared getting something "bad" in my mouth. "Honey," she said, "when I was a little girl, I also went through a stage of spitting frequently. I got over it, and you will, too. You should not worry about getting something bad in your mouth."

This comment took the onus off me, and I felt more comfortable now that I knew that my mother had shared this strange predilection. Shortly after that, my spitting fixation ceased to exist, and it was forgotten. I give my mother the credit for that. This episode was possibly my first real experience with obsessive-compulsive behavior.

When I was in the third grade, my leg began hurting while I was walking to the school cafeteria. It was a mild pain and probably wouldn't have upset the average child. I began to imagine that this pain in my leg was a sure symptom of some awful, life-threatening illness. I broke out in a cold sweat and felt weak all over. The thoughts of a dreadful disease wouldn't go away; they kept swirling around in my head until, after an hour, I was in acute mental anguish and near panic. I finally worked up the courage to tell my teacher that I was very sick, and in a trembling voice, I asked if she could please call my mother to come and get me. The teacher, probably noticing the agonized look on my face, did as I asked, and about twenty minutes later Mama arrived at school and took me home. She asked me what was wrong, and I told her that my leg hurt. She replied, in her usual consoling manner, "Reagan, it's probably nothing to worry about; more than likely, it's just a muscle ache, and if it goes away soon, we won't worry about it." Those words from my mother comforted me, and soon the pain was gone and forgotten. But I had experienced my first encounter with irrational terror.

Over the next few years, I often became fearful that I was surely going to contract a terrible illness. At night, my mother would tuck me into bed, and I would often tell her that I feared I was going to become ill with some sickness or other. She would pat me on the head and say, "The doctor says that you're as healthy as a horse, and you're going to stay that way." These reassuring words from my mother would always put my mind at ease. I would fall asleep and not worry about that particular illness again, but a week or a month later, another phantom illness would invade my happiness, and the misery would start again.

My mother was always ready to help, and she could always comfort me in those early years when I would confide in her about my bizarre thoughts. Many a night she would sit beside me on my bed, and I would begin, "Mama, I'm worrying again."

Throughout my young years I worried and worried and worried. I even worried because I was worrying so much, and I confronted my mother with this. She said, "Your best friend's mother tells me that he sometimes worries about catching a disease, too." It made me happy at the time to find out that I was not the only boy who spent time worrying. This newly acquired knowledge made me think that it was normal for small children to worry a lot, and I began believing that I was no different from most kids. Not much later I came to the realization that I was, indeed, very different from other children.

In the fall of 1957, when I was in the seventh grade, my parents built a new house that was located close to the one we had lived in for some time. Shortly after we moved into the new house, something peculiar began to happen. I started feeling worried most of the time, but not about contracting an illness. I just seemed to feel worried for no reason. I discussed this feeling with my mother on one occasion. This uncomfortable feeling went on for several months, but I never discussed it with my mother again. I didn't feel comfortable talking about the strangeness that I was experiencing. I didn't understand this, and I didn't know how to explain it. So I suffered in silence. Not long after this experience, I began to undergo my first full-blown obsessive-compulsive symptoms.

One night, I was eating dinner, but I wasn't very hungry, so I didn't clean my plate. After I left the table, my mother noticed that there was still food left on my plate. She told me to go back to the table and finish eating. I became angry and stalked off to my bedroom. My mother didn't follow me to scold, so I knew that I had won. Suddenly, a very powerful urge overtook me. It told me to go back to the table and clean my plate as my mother had instructed. I was confused. I wondered why I was thinking this. I didn't want to go back to the kitchen and eat the rest of my food. But the urge, the compulsion, wouldn't die! It became increasingly more powerful. I was about twelve at the time and didn't know what a neurotic compulsion was. These words were not a part of my vocabulary. All I knew was that this strange, unwelcome, and terrifying thought was controlling me, and I had to obey it.

Suddenly, another unsettling thought overcame me. What if my mother had already thrown the food away? This thought was horrifying. I broke out in a sweat and, trembling, rushed back to the kitchen. There was my plate, still on the table. I felt such relief. The last thing I wanted at this time was food. But I obeyed the terrible compulsion. I sat down at my plate and began eating the rest of my food. I practically had to force the food down my throat. I wasn't hungry. I did not want to eat. Hadn't I just been victorious over my mother concerning our dispute? Now something was telling me that I had to eat this food that I didn't want. Consuming the unwanted food made me gag several times, but I dutifully sat there at my plate, controlled by a terrifying and mysterious force, eating until every morsel was gone. Confused and frightened, I returned to my bedroom, knowing that what had transpired wasn't normal. In the past I had confided troubling thoughts to my mother. But this was different. I knew that I didn't dare tell my mother or anyone else of this experience. Voicing this, I feared, might lead to some dreadful consequences.

One night a few months later, I removed my clothes and shoes and crawled into bed. There was a night light in the hall beside my room, and as I lay in bed, I noticed that my shoes weren't lined up perfectly side by side. Suddenly this began to bother me. Then I chastised myself thinking that I was silly to worry about shoes. Nothing like this had ever upset me before. I realized that I was experiencing another abnormal thought, and this realization frightened me even more. I tried to go to sleep, but I just couldn't stop thinking about those shoes. I had a compulsion to get out of bed and line them up exactly beside each other. I tried to resist the thought, but the harder I resisted, the more powerful the thought became.

I wished that I could just forget the shoes and go to sleep. I could not. I was a prisoner of my own thinking. After an hour of internal struggle, I timidly crawled out of bed and straightened my shoes. In a way, I felt relief, yet I also felt defeated. I had surrendered again to thoughts I knew to be irrational.

I was becoming more and more aware that something very wrong was happening to me. I knew I dared not tell my mother or anyone else. I wondered if I was going crazy. Why would a person feel compelled to do things he really did not want to do? I knew that crazy people were put into insane asylums, some for the remainder of their lives. I thought that, if I told someone what I had been experiencing, there was a chance I would be taken to one of those horrible places where people were put in straitjackets. I could not risk it. I could never tell!

Another notable incident concerning shoes occurred around this same time period. For numerous years I had dreamed of and longed for a real pair of metal-spiked baseball shoes. One day my dream came true. Mama took me to town and let me pick out and buy a pair of baseball spikes. I was elated! Upon arriving home, I hurriedly slipped the new shoes onto my feet, then ran around the front yard like a crazed baseball player, sharply dodging this way and that and having the time of my life.

My joy wasn't long lasting. That night as I sat in the family room of our house staring happily at the baseball shoes sitting near the wall, my happiness suddenly, mysteriously turned to anguish. I began to become anxious. Abruptly the sight of the beloved baseball shoes became disconcerting. I became confused and shaken. Why would the object of my happiness suddenly create unpleasant emotions in me? A few moments before I had been the happiest kid alive. Now I was rapidly becoming one of the most miserable. The baseball shoes had turned on me and become my villain, and I felt myself growing to despise them. None of the new feelings made sense, but one thing was sure. Although I was staring at the same baseball shoes that had earlier brought happiness, now, for some unexplainable reason, they were producing agitation and sorrow. I had a feeling of unworthiness. The unwelcome emotions gradually faded with time, and over the years I enjoyed the baseball shoes on numerous occasions. But to this day, I can't explain the feelings of overwhelming morose that overtook me on that night which should have been one of the happiest times of my life.

There was another instance of a negative emotional response being perpetrated in me after I received something brand new.

My great aunt Mae was a very thoughtful and loving person. Though she lived far away, she always remembered my sister and me on our birthdays and at Christmas. One Christmas season when I was thirteen, I became ill with the flu and missed several days of school. On my first day at home, a package arrived from my aunt. When I opened my present, I discovered that it was a kit for building a small Christmas reindeer out of Styrofoam, wooden sticks, and ribbons. I was overjoyed! I loved to build things and put things together. I ripped open the box and began to work assembling the little deer. I was enjoying myself and thinking how much I loved my aunt Mae. I attached the Styrofoam head to a wooden stick. Then I stuck four wooden legs into the Styrofoam body of the deer. I connected the head, added sequin eyes, then decorated the body by wrapping red ribbons around it. The last step was to attach a green bow that was to be the deer's tail. I pushed the long straight pin with the bow connected to it into the rear end of the deer's body. Then it happened! Suddenly, I felt an overpowering urge to remove the pin from the deer's rear end. I thought how crazy this was. I had just had a great time creating a Christmas decoration, and now I could not resist this overpowering need to remove the deer's tail. The more I resisted, the more commanding the feeling became. I became nervous and distraught.

There was no mistaking it now. I was losing my mind, and there was nothing that I could do about it. My situation seemed hopeless. I was desperate, and I hated that deer. If I removed the tail, I would be giving in to this insane urge, and that would be defeat. I could not stop the intrusive thoughts, but this time I did not yield. For the rest of the day, the deer and its bow for a tail were all my troubled mind would focus upon. That night, I slept fitfully, frequently awakening, and always with the terrible need to unpin the deer's tail. Once during the night my mother came and put her cheek against my forehead. Upon finding it damp, she remarked that I must be recovering from the flu because my fever had broken. What she did not know was that the perspiration was a result of the deep mental anxiety and agony that I was experiencing.

The next day was not better. The persistent thoughts continued. I tried my best to behave normally. For three long days and nights the terrible thoughts allowed me only intermittent sleep. However, I steadfastly resisted the compulsion to remove the deer's tail, and all through the ordeal I felt emotionally spent and exhausted. At this point, I thought that to succumb to the impulse would constitute an admission that I was hopelessly insane and unable to control my own thoughts and actions.

I finally recovered from the flu and went back to school. Christmas came and went, and my mother put the deer away and out of sight; this was a blessing and a relief. But for several years, whenever I thought about the toy deer, I felt an urge to remove its tail.

OCD was firmly entrenched in my mind by the age of fourteen. My sister Sheila had been away to college for two years. One day while in Sheila's room, I was looking through the N volume of our encyclopedia and accidentally ran across the unfamiliar word *neurosis*. I read a paragraph out of curiosity. I was shocked! The paragraph described neurosis as a type of mental illness in which people sometimes thought thoughts that they didn't want to think and did things they didn't want to do. The article used other unfamiliar words: *obsession* and *compulsion*.

I immediately unmistakably recognized myself fitting the mold of a person with this mental illness. The symptoms described in the article paralleled mine exactly. I now knew positively that I was mentally ill. The encyclopedia article disturbed me so much that I didn't finish reading it.

I reached the decision that I must continue to suffer in silence, for I believed that, if I ever let my condition become known, I was doomed to spend the rest of my life in a mental institution. To me that would be the worst thing that could happen to a person. I was familiar with stories of shock therapy, straitjackets, and rubber rooms. They terrified me. I visualized mentally ill people's being locked up in insane asylums, never to be visited by loved ones or friends. I was well aware of the terrible stigma attached to a person who was "insane," and I knew relatives were sometimes ashamed even to talk about them. I wondered why it was OK to have a physical illness like cancer or heart disease, but not a mental illness.

I was intensely ashamed of myself for being mentally ill. I felt that I was a defective, flawed individual. I didn't want my loved ones to be ashamed of me. I believed it was better to suffer in silence than to be found out and put away!

I recall becoming terrified of even the word *insane*. Once at about the age of fifteen, I was looking through the dictionary when my eyes accidentally fell upon this particular word. I bolted upright and almost jumped out of my skin! I felt blood rush to my face, and my heart pounded in my chest. My whole body felt shocked and numb. Just the appearance of this word jolted me as if a high voltage of electricity had surged through my body. I later wondered how just a simple word in the dictionary could hold such incredible power over me. But it did!

Ten years later I was in a branch of the Dallas Public Library; I looked up the word *neuroses* in a book concerning mental health. I'll never forget what the article said about people with OCD: "These poor unfortunate individuals generally cannot be cured by chemical treatment or psychotherapy, and they are usually doomed to unproductive lives of misery and agony."

I felt as if all hope was gone. I had a non-treatable, incurable disease, and I was destined to a life of torment and suffering.

2 THE PIG PEN

I was raised on a farm. Early in my junior high days, I told my parents that I would like to raise hogs for the livestock show in Mercedes. They liked the idea, and Daddy built me a pen about one hundred yards west of our house. He placed a concrete slab at one end of the pen so that during rainy weather the pig would have a place that wasn't muddy. The concrete slab covered about one fourth of the pen.

One side of the slab had a chunk of concrete knocked out of it, and a small pig could possibly have escaped from the pen through that hole. I located a block of concrete of about the right size to fill in the hole. It became my habit, when feeding my pig, to stand on the block of concrete and reach over the side of the pen to pour the feed into the trough.

One rainy day, I noticed that my shoes left some mud on the block, so I used one of my shoes to scrape the mud from it. The next time it rained, I repeated this procedure of scraping the mud off the block with my shoe, but I did not get all the mud off, so I repeated the process. On the next rainy day, I scraped mud from the block with one shoe, then felt compelled to repeat the procedure with the other shoe. Soon, I began noticing that, even when it was not muddy, my shoes left dirt on the block.

Before long, every time I fed my pig, I would perform the dirt-removing ritual, and it slowly became more involved. I would scrape the block with my right shoe twice, then with my left shoe twice. If I did not do it quite right, I would have to begin again. This second time it would be once with the right shoe, twice with the left shoe, then again with the right shoe. There had to be equality and symmetry! If I did not do the ritual to my satisfaction, I'd have to begin again from the start, but this next time everything would be doubled. So I would scrape twice with the right, four with the left, and twice more with the right. Then my hands became involved. After the feet had finished, the hands would repeat the procedure. Then feet and hands would alternate: one round with the feet, two rounds with the hands, and another with the feet. The worst thing was, if I did not do it perfectly, I had to start over from the beginning and double my efforts.

The longer the ritual would last, the more anxious I would become; the more anxious I would become, the more inclined I was to "mess up" and have to start over. There were times when the concrete block ritual lasted for over two hours! At those times the ritual would become so complicated that it required a good memory on my part to remember all the facets of the ritual and do them perfectly.

Feeding the pig became the daily activity that I dreaded most. Plus I was constantly aware that all this was insane. This was so crazy that I would ask myself, "Why am I doing this?" But I felt as if I had to do it. If I missed one time performing the ritual, I would be continuously uncomfortable, always with the persistent, gnawing urge to go to the pig pen and perform the ritual. I also would not be able to sleep well that night. I might spend all night with the obsession in my mind to wipe the dirt off that concrete block.

I had lost sleep because of obsessions and compulsions in the past, and the consequence of skipping a ritual was terribly fearful to me--so much so that I avoided it whenever possible like a plague. It was as if the concrete block had a magical control over me, as if it owned me. Possessed me! It was eerie. I wanted nothing more in the world than to cease this ritual, but I had to carry out this ritual every time I fed the pig, and it was driving me crazy. I hated to feed the pig!

Our tractor driver's kids, Raul and Lupe, fed a calf at the calf pen about forty yards north of the pig pen. I would often ask them to feed the pig for me, and said I would feed the calf for them. I was unaccustomed to feeding the calf, so I had no obsessions, compulsions, or rituals concerning its feeding. I could carry feed to the calf pen and dump it into the food container, and that would be that. When I fed my pig, I had to go through all this ritual stuff. Therefore, I would frequently try to convince Raul and Lupe to switch jobs with me. I never offered any explanation about why I wanted to switch. They were usually willing to switch, but I think that, after many switches, they began to wonder if I was being devious. Maybe they were getting the harder of the two jobs. However, the calf pen was farther away, and the feed had to be carried a longer distance. Nevertheless, at times they did not want to switch, and at those times I would literally beg them to feed the pig. I am sure they thought my behavior was strange, but they usually cooperated.

There was a road beside the pig pen. A small irrigation canal ran parallel to it, and a deep drainage ditch ran parallel to the canal. I wanted to take that concrete block and hurl it into the drainage ditch! But I could not. I would think, "I cannot do that to that concrete block." It was truly as if the block had control over me, as though it had its own life. I would think about its sinking down in the mud in the bottom of the drainage ditch, and I could visualize myself feeling sorry for it. I felt as if I would be killing it. I did not want to hurt it. I wanted to get rid of it, but I did not want to hurt it! I imagined that, if I threw it to the bottom of the drainage ditch, then every night after that for the rest of my life I would be obsessed with the thought that it was lying at the bottom of the ditch and could never be recovered. The concrete block had become an animate object to me; I thought of it as though it were alive. It was all so very bizarre.

On one occasion when I was performing the concrete block ritual, a pickup truck drove past me before I noticed. I was sure that the man inside the pickup had seen me doing the ritual. I became terrified! I had been found out. Somebody now knew that I was crazy. I became enormously paranoid. All I could think about was being "found out." He might tell my parents what he had seen, and I would be committed to one of those horrible insane asylums.

In retrospect, I am sure that the man in the pickup truck had no idea what I was doing, but at the time I became very distraught. I never saw the man again, and nothing except my siege of fear ever came of the incident.

The concrete block ritual at the pig pen was not the only time I associated life with something nonliving. I seemed to have feelings toward other inanimate objects--feelings such as sorrow, joy, etc. I began to experience these feelings for objects like pencils and shoes. I had feelings for them and began to think that they too had feelings. I knew this was extremely weird and abnormal. I also knew that it was not true; despite how hard I tried not to have these feelings and thoughts, I could not halt them. I thought thoughts that I did not want to think, but I could not help thinking them. They flooded into my consciousness, and I could not control them. They invaded my mind whether I liked them or not!

3 THE PAIN OF NOT KNOWING

During my eighth grade school year, my English teacher, Mrs. Rapp, instructed the class to read a short story entitled "The Lady or the Tiger?" by Frank R. Stockton. This story had an enormous impact upon my obsessive-compulsive mind.

The story takes place in olden times and concerns a semibarbaric king who practiced an uncommon method of justice when dealing with his subjects. When a subject was accused of some impropriety, he was brought into a large arena surrounded by a multitude of spectators.

The arena contained two identical doors at one end. Behind one of the doors was a ferocious, hungry tiger, the most vicious man-eater that could be found. Behind the other door sat a fair lady.

The accused was required to open one of the doors. If the accused opened the door with the tiger, the ravenous monster would immediately spring upon its victim and tear him to pieces. If, however, the accused opened the door with the fair lady, he and the lady would be immediately married by a priest (whether the accused was agreeable or not).

The king had a daughter who was the apple of his eye. She was beautiful and, like her father, a bit barbaric. The princess had a lover, unbeknownst to the king. The lover was one of the handsomest and bravest young men in the kingdom.

When the king found out about his daughter's lover, he was determined to end the affair. This was the first time in the kingdom's history that a princess had had a subject for a lover. The king decided to send the young man to the arena and thereby rid himself of the problem.

With the benefit of some pieces of gold, the princess was able to do something that had never been accomplished before: she was able to learn the secret of what would be behind each door. She also learned what lady would be behind one of the doors, and it was a beautiful young girl of whom the princess was very jealous. She had seen her lover with this woman on a couple of occasions. She hated this woman. But she loved her lover. She would rather anything else happen than for her lover to fall into the arms of this other woman. However, she couldn't bear the thought of seeing her lover slain by the tiger.

The day arrived for the king's justice to be served. The arena was packed. The young man walked into the arena, and he peered at the princess sitting next to her father. Since the two lovers were as one, he read the look on her face and realized that she knew the secret of the doors. He stared at her questioningly. She, without anyone else's noticing, pointed to the right-hand door.

Then the story ends with this question, "Which came out the door--the lady or the tiger?"

When I read that question, I felt as if my mind had exploded! I was jolted to the bone. I became dazed and couldn't speak or concentrate on anything except the unanswered question in the story. I felt numb and in pain--horrible mental pain--pain caused by not knowing the ending of the story. My mind begged for a conclusion. It begged for closure but found none. I HAD to know which came out of the door! But the story had no ending! My mind couldn't cope with that fact. Although for someone who has never experienced this it is hard to understand, for OCD victims, such is the nature of life.

For the rest of that day and for the next three days, I could think of nothing except that story. That awful story was making me crazy.

I remember that the next day I went on a school trip to a volleyball tournament. I walked around the other school's campus feeling dazed and stunned; I was in mental turmoil, my mind constantly seeking closure to the story. All I could think of was that story and the ghastly, gnawing emotional vacuum it had left in my mind.

How could just a simple story in an eighth-grade literature book cause such agony? It was astonishing!

4 HIGH SCHOOL "MADNESS"

I played basketball in high school. The night before a game I would pack my basketball uniform and shoes into a tote bag. My OCD caused me to pack my bag meticulously, but I would also pack it quickly.

One autumn day our basketball squad traveled to the small town of Riviera to play a game against their high school team. When I went into the locker room to change into my basketball uniform, I found to my chagrin that I had failed to pack my basketball shoes. I confronted the coach with this dilemma. He stated, "Well, absent-minded Reagan forgot something again."

Fortunately, I found an old pair of basketball shoes of the right size in the visitors' locker room.

A few days later, Sherman Click, a teammate of mine, gave me some advice: "Reagan, I always double check my tote bag after I have packed it, to be sure all my basketball stuff is packed."

I didn't tell Sherman, but packing my tote bag was an activity that troubled me. I wanted everything to be arranged perfectly. The normal anxiety brought about by an upcoming game probably made my OCD more acute. I wanted to place everything into the bag precisely but quickly. I wanted to pack rapidly because I didn't want any excess time in which to ponder this activity for fear of becoming caught up in an involved OCD ritual. I would NEVER double check the contents of the bag because I feared that I might find something out of place and that it would aggravate my OCD. If I did find something amiss, I feared I would have to stand there for an extended period trying to get everything positioned perfectly. I didn't want the packing of my tote bag to become ritualized. The pig pen ritual had left me with the lasting dread of becoming involved in further rituals.

I was frequently accused of being absent-minded in those days. I received considerable teasing and ridicule from teachers and fellow students for displaying absent-mindedness. And I was absent-minded. I was absent-minded because I was frequently preoccupied with the obsessive and compulsive thoughts that were cluttering my mind and forcing other thoughts out. My mind was so fixated upon irrational thoughts and behaviors that I was often absent-minded about remembering those things which were truly important.

* * *

One afternoon I borrowed Daddy's pickup truck and drove a few miles to visit a friend. My father had some farm equipment in the back of his pickup, and on the way over to the friend's house, unbeknownst to me, a heavy chain slid out of the bed of the pickup and onto the road. Traveling home, I noticed a chain lying on the road as I passed by. I suspected that it might be my father's chain. No matter the ownership, most people would have stopped to pick up the chain, since these heavy chains were somewhat expensive and the road was an uncrowded farm road.

But I didn't stop. I thought about stopping. But I was so involved in neurotic rituals in those days that even the apparently simple act of stopping and retrieving a chain might trigger my OCD. I knew I couldn't just pick up the chain and load it into the bed of the pickup as a normal person would. I knew I would become obsessed with some small detail of this simple action, and I would suffer some type of obsessive-compulsive "pain." That is how sick I was. I was so sick that I couldn't even perform a seemingly simple action without paying a high price.

Later at home my father informed me that a chain was missing from the bed of his pickup, and he asked if I had seen it. I replied that on my way home I had noticed a chain lying on the road, but I hadn't picked it up. My father heatedly exclaimed, "You didn't pick it up? Why not? It was my chain. Even if you didn't know who lost it, you should have picked it up." My father very seldom became angry with me, but on this occasion he was livid.

* * *

While in high school, I got into the habit of lingering in doorways. I don't know what brought this ritual about except that, like all OCD rituals, it was anxiety related.

Each doorway into a classroom had a metal strip along the bottom fixed onto the wooden floor. As I would enter the threshold, I would hesitate; I would concentrate my weight upon the metal strip with my left foot and then upon my right foot for perfect symmetry. Then I would enter the room. (I guess this ritual was an offshoot of the pig pen ritual.) Once a fellow student questioned this behavior. As I was pausing on the threshold of the door leading into the library, a schoolmate named Melba asked, "Reagan, why do you linger in doorways?"

I was stunned! Melba had noticed my unusual behavior. "I didn't realize that I did," I replied.

To my great relief, she dropped the subject. No one could find out about my secret illness, or in my mind I would be one step closer to an insane asylum.

My first girlfriend was Malda, the daughter of my parents' best friends. She was in the fourth grade, and I in the sixth when I had fallen for her. While in high school, Malda and I remained good friends and dated occasionally. Meanwhile, I had developed the ritual of tapping first one foot and then the other several times on the bottom door frame of a car before I would step from the automobile. On one particular date with Malda, I had pulled the car into her driveway, and we sat there for a time talking before she had to go into her house. I opened my car door and, as was my custom, tapped first one foot, then the other, on the bottom door frame. Before I could exit the automobile, Malda questioned, "Why do you do that?"

I froze! I was being found out. I replied something about, "I'm removing the dirt from my shoes." Malda didn't pursue the subject, but I was becoming nervous that people around me were beginning to notice too much!

I had made good grades my freshman and sophomore years in high school. Due to overwhelming OCD, my grades fell off my junior year. Toward the end of that year, Mrs. Virginia Guess, my English teacher, asked me, "Why have your grades taken a dip this year, Reagan? You used to be such a good student."

I can't remember what lie I voiced to counter her charge, but I always quickly thought of halfway plausible explanations.

My junior year in high school was one of the most hellish years of my life. My OCD became so severe that I could barely function. There were two things that kept me going: one was my strong faith in the Lord, and the other was a girl named Carol.* Early that year I had met her. She was a slender fifteen-year-old brunette who attended the same church as a friend of mine. I had accompanied him to church one day and was introduced to Carol. I thought she was beautiful, and I couldn't get her out of my mind.

We had met only once; I barely knew her, and yet I thought of her every day. Dwight, our mutual friend, would report to me about Carol each time he saw her at

---

*name changed

church. I could hardly wait to see him on Mondays and Thursdays to find out about her. My infatuation went beyond reason and bordered on obsession. I have never before or since had such a crush on a human being whom I scarcely knew.

At this time, OCD was controlling my life to such an extent that I performed numerous rituals every day. I remember thinking that I was very sick, but that I could endure all because my love for Carol would cancel out the unhappiness. My thoughts of her were all consuming, and I felt that I could survive anything just for the joy that her memory brought to my mind. Although I had never talked to her more than five minutes, she was always with me. Her existence in my mind made my tortured life tolerable.

Toward the end of my junior year, a wonderful event occurred. The junior-senior prom was rapidly approaching, and I needed a date. I didn't know Carol's phone number, so I asked Dwight if he would ask Carol if she would be my date to the prom. He did, and she accepted my invitation. I was elated! I was actually going to have a date with the girl I worshipped. It seemed too good to be true.

I will never forget the prom day. I was so preoccupied with OCD and so exuberant over my date that I completely forgot to buy a corsage for her. I remembered it about fifteen minutes before the stores closed. We lived five miles out in the country, and I was horrified. I will never forget what my father did for me that day. He rushed to a flower shop only a few minutes before it closed and returned home a half hour later with flowers for Carol!

I got into the bathtub with plenty of time to take a bath and dress before I went to pick Carol up and drive to the prom. (She lived rather far away, and I would have to drive about thirty miles before we reached the prom.) I was so anxious about the date with the girl of my dreams that I performed many rituals in the bath.

Performing rituals while taking a bath was nothing new. I did it all the time and had been doing it for years. I would wash one arm, then the other arm twice, then the first arm again. The same with the legs, ears, toes, etc. And there were numerous ramifications of these rites. If I messed up, I would have to start over from the beginning. I always washed the parts of my body in the exact same order.

But now I was going to have a date with Carol. I had daydreamed about her for almost a whole year, yet I had spoken to her only a time or two. So high was my anxiety that I performed four to five times as many rituals in the bathtub that day as I ordinarily did. My bath required almost two hours to complete. The longer it took, the more nervous I became about being late for my date and the more rituals I had to perform. Finally, I was able to lift myself from the tub, dress, and leave the house. My hair was cut very short in those days. I remember driving away without combing it, so preoccupied and rushed was I.

Carol looked stunning in her formal gown. Unbelievably, we were only a few minutes late to the prom. I had a wonderful time. After the prom Carol, another couple, and I drove to my house where my mother served us refreshments and took home movies of us. As I drove Carol home, I was in a happy never-never land.

Two to three weeks later I summoned the courage to ask my friend Dwight if he would talk to Carol about going out with me again. I will never forget his reply the next day. "Reagan," he said, "Carol told me to inform you that she has just begun to go steady with someone else, but she thanks you for the invitation anyway!"

I was crushed! Upon receiving the news, I staggered out of my parents' house and wandered along the nearby irrigation canal bank, crying like a baby all the while. I must have wept for thirty to forty minutes.

Several years later I saw Carol in a department store, and we greeted each other. Although the dream was gone, I remembered the thoughts and anguish I had experienced. That was the last time I laid eyes on her.

Maybe my obsessional love for her served a good purpose. It had occurred during a year when my life otherwise would have been nothing short of total misery. Had not my thoughts of Carol given me something to live for, I would surely have had an even more difficult struggle with life.

The following summer I went into a remission so powerful that I felt normal and behaved almost normally for three years. I was to win enough respect from my school peers that in my senior year I was elected class president, class favorite, and captain of the varsity basketball team. How much difference a single year can make!

5 OUR FATHER WHO ART IN HEAVEN

I was raised in a Christian home. My great-grandfather on my mother's side was a Baptist minister. I remember old photographs of him with his long white beard. My maternal grandmother, a preacher's daughter, was a very devout Christian.

My father was raised a Methodist, and my mother began attending the Methodist Church with him after they were married. Throughout my life at home, our family attended church faithfully. Church was a very important part of our lives.

I have always had the habit of praying before going to sleep at night. When I began to become emotionally disturbed as a child, I began praying for healing from the affliction. I prayed hard for many years, and I experienced varying degrees of periodic mental illness and remission during my early youth.

When I began developing severe OCD symptoms at the beginning of adolescence, transistor radios were just becoming a popular item on the market. I bought one and kept it on the headboard of my bed. I accidentally discovered a radio station that broadcast Billy Graham's sermons nightly, and almost every night for years, I fell asleep listening to his preaching. I became a very strong believer. Although much time through the years in junior high school and high school was spent battling moderate to severe mental illness, my faith in the Lord remained unshakable. I firmly believed that in good times or bad He would see me through. I continued to pray earnestly for healing every night.

During one particularly bad OCD period that lasted a couple of years, my favorite time of the day was bedtime because this was the time when the suffering of the day was over and blissful sleep ensued. For those eight hours of sleep, I was released from the throes of the agonizing OCD that tormented me during my waking hours. Yet I remained faithful to the Lord and ever hopeful that someday He would release me from this living hell. Even if I never found relief from mental illness while on this earth, I was convinced that wonderful peace and happiness were awaiting me in the hereafter. I felt sure that I needed only to remain a faithful servant of the Lord to gain this victory. I was always confident in my mind that the Lord was compassionate and merciful to mentally ill individuals like me, that He knew exactly what suffering we were enduring, and that someday we would receive our release and our reward.

As I have mentioned, the worst year of my early life was my junior year in high school. But a miracle happened that summer. I became mentally normal. This was an indescribable blessing! And the change happened very quickly. I had the best year of my high school days my senior year. I was so normal that Sue, my steady girlfriend during that period, never knew or suspected anything unusual about my mental health.

6 OFF TO COLLEGE

My freshman and sophomore years in college seemed wonderful. I redefined my attitudes and, to a certain degree, my ideas of human morality. For example, in high school, the idea of having premarital sex was incompatible with my upbringing and my strong relationship with the Lord. I had never drunk alcohol while in high school. I believed drinking to be wrong; although many of my friends drank, I refused to partake.

During my sophomore year in college, however, I did indulge in premarital sex. I also discovered alcohol and began to drink occasionally. Several times I got drunk. I almost completely stopped going to church. I was normal now; my life was under control, and I somewhat forgot God.

I became like the farmer who was repairing the roof of his barn. Beginning to slip, he became fearful, and desperately prayed, "Lord! Save me! Save me!" Then his pants caught on a nail, and he said, "Oh, never mind, Lord. I'm caught on a nail."

During my first two years in college, I believed my mental illness was a thing of the past that would never recur. My life was now mine to live any way I wanted, and I chose many wrong paths.

Then, as suddenly as it had improved, my mental health came crashing down during the first semester of my junior year in college.

I had developed the routine of going to the college library each night to study, and my grades reflected this practice. Toward the end of the semester, I had an A average in all my courses--difficult courses, such as trigonometry, chemistry, and history. One night in the library, as I was studying my handwritten class notes, I noticed that one of my letters was not written properly. It was the letter *a*, and it was not closed at the top. Another person would never have noticed this, but this imperfection hit me like a bombshell. Suddenly I had the terrible urge to change the letter. I had never been obsessed with handwriting before. I fought the compulsion with all my strength and tried desperately not to yield to it.

I was terrified! I had been in a remission from mental illness since my senior year in high school. I had considered my mental illness a thing of the past. I was normal now, just like everyone else. How could this be happening?

I tried to skip over the word with the imperfect letter and continue studying. Then I noticed other letters that were not perfect. (Of course, while note taking during class, my handwriting was fast and scribbled.) I noticed letter after letter that was imperfect. I had a sudden driving impulse to change these letters, but I would not let myself because I knew this would be "crazy." I did not want to be crazy! Not again! Knowing that the compulsion itself was "crazy" made me extremely anxious, and the anxiety drove the compulsion on even stronger.

"Why me?" I thought. "How could this be happening, just when everything is going so wonderfully?" But happen it did! I quickly sank back down into the grip of debilitating illness. I did not manually change any of the imperfect letters on this occasion, but after that, whenever I wrote, I felt strongly compelled to "correct" any letters that did not seem just right.

The result was that I blew my final exams because I was so concerned with my handwriting that I could not concentrate on studying. Due to the low grades that resulted from my failing my final exams, the college placed me on scholastic probation for the next semester. I was heartsick. I had had dreams of going to medical school, and I watched them vanish in the distance. I entered into a state of deep depression due to my bashed dreams and my reawakened insanity!

I came home for semester break and told my parents that I wanted to drop out of college and go to work. I did not provide them with a good reason. They went to see my old pediatrician; he advised them to persuade me to see a psychiatrist. I ignored this advice. I knew the doctor was right, but I did not want to risk spending the remainder of my life in a mental hospital.

Two years later a related incident occurred. When I worked as a laboratory technician at Southwestern Medical School in Dallas, I was often asked to write a doctor's name on a 3" by 5" card and attach it to a cage of laboratory rats. This simple activity should have taken seconds, but there were times when I secretly labored for ten to fifteen minutes and went through several cards before I was able to write the name to my neurotic mind's satisfaction.

Several years later, my first psychiatrist asked me what would happen if I did not perform a ritual or yield to a compulsion. I did not answer his question. I was somewhat embarrassed to admit that, if I failed to do these things, I would often become so preoccupied with the troubling thoughts that I would lie awake all night with numerous obsessive-compulsive preoccupations swirling through my mind. This consequence was so utterly unpleasant and fearful that I always tried to avoid it at all costs!

Interestingly, even today I am not comfortable with my handwriting. I still try to make my letters just right, and occasionally, if I do not make a letter just right, I have to change it. However, I do not now sit and agonize about this. I just go ahead, change the letter, and move on.

7 DIRTY DISHES AND COLOR TV

I married my girlfriend, Debbie, when we were both very young. We lived in an apartment in Denton, Texas, for two years while I finished working toward my bachelor's degree at the University of North Texas.

My first child, Brian, was born at Baylor Hospital in Dallas in the fall of 1967. Upon her dismissal from the hospital after Brian's birth, Debbie stayed in Dallas with her parents for approximately two weeks.

On the day Debbie had gone into labor, we had rushed off to Dallas and left behind a sink full of dirty dishes. Returning home two weeks later, Debbie discovered that I had not washed any of the dishes, and she didn't let me live this down for a long time. Some of the dishes still had food on them, with green and gray mold growing prolifically. Like my parents and everyone else at that time, Debbie did not know that I suffered from mental illness.

Debbie asked why I hadn't washed the dishes. I made up a feeble excuse that sounded halfway credible: "I was too busy studying to wash them." She was understandably upset. She didn't know the real reason I hadn't washed the dirty dishes.

I wouldn't allow myself to wash dishes or perform other such tasks because doing so might activate the OCD. I thought, if I didn't wash them to suit my perfectionist tendency, I would become anxious and have to perform numerous rituals. I feared that even a simple task like washing dishes might lead to sleepless nights with obsessed thoughts that I hadn't done it correctly. I already found it hard enough to take notes and study with the perfectionist handwriting preoccupation, and I didn't want any additional aggravation.

I graduated from college in August of 1969. Shortly before that date I had begun working at Southwestern Medical School in Dallas during the day and at Brown Express at night. At that time color television sets were just beginning to become popular and affordable, and Debbie and I purchased one. We watched a war movie that first night and were captivated by the beauty of the "color." I had dreamed for many years of owning a color TV, and now I finally owned one. I was elated!

My ecstasy was short lived. While watching TV on the second night, I noticed a small red power-on light illuminated at the base of the set. Before long, every time I watched TV, I became distracted by this light. I couldn't stop glancing at it. I kept wishing it wasn't there. Why it bothered me I can't exactly say. The light was small -- about the size of two grains of rice, and it protruded a few millimeters. Within days I became so obsessed with the little red light that I couldn't concentrate on watching TV. My eyes were constantly drawn to that red light.

Now my wonderful color television set, which I had looked forward to buying for so many years, was a villain. Instead of watching it with enjoyment, I was becoming miserable. After about a week, I told Debbie that I had decided that we really couldn't afford the set and that I wanted to return it to the store. I lied. Debbie could not be told the truth. No one must know about my illness.

Surprisingly, Debbie voiced no objection to returning the TV. She even called the store and asked the salesman who had sold us the set to come and pick it up, saying, to my recollection, that we weren't satisfied with the quality of the picture. The salesman brought two other TV sets to our apartment, but my troubled mind found something "wrong" with both of them. The salesman took all three sets back to the store, and our money was refunded. Secretly, I was very appreciative to Debbie for not objecting to returning the set. I felt victorious and defeated at the same time. But mostly, I felt defeated!

Billye, Debbie's mother, had bought Debbie and me a huge, expensive white Bible. We kept it on our coffee table. Later, Debbie and I separated for a month. During the separation, Brian, now three years old, tore a page out of the Bible. Debbie showed it to me when we got back together. Privately, I was horrified, but I tried desperately not to show it. This was the *Good Book*, and in my way of thinking, it had been "violated." Naturally, I knew that a three year old couldn't be held accountable for his actions, so I wasn't angry with my young son. But what was I to do? I felt intensely uncomfortable with the torn-out page just lying there inside the Bible. At the same time, I couldn't throw the torn page away, for this was part of a sacred book; to my neurotic mind, to throw a page away would be akin to sacrilege. My mind also desperately wanted to tear out the remnant of the torn page still attached to the Bible, but I couldn't do this either. It would "violate" the *Good Book*!

I was trapped in a "Catch 22." The torn page in the Bible troubled me for months. Even though I was very sorrowful when Debbie and I went our separate ways a few months later, I was relieved about one thing. When she left to move in with her mother, she took the Bible with her. I was getting away from the Bible with the torn page, and to me out of sight was out of mind. For some crazy reason, if the Bible wasn't physically present any longer, I didn't "need" to feel any more anxiety about the torn page. It was as if this was now someone else's problem, and I didn't have to be troubled about it anymore.

Little did I know that these OCD symptoms concerning the color TV and the Bible were probably the result of the anxiety spawned by a crumbling marriage.

8 MARRIAGE WOES

My marriage to Debbie was happy for about three years as far as I was concerned. We moved to Dallas shortly after my graduation from the University of North Texas. Early in our marriage, I had gone into a partial remission from mental illness. I had begun work at two jobs. I was required to join the Teamster's Union before reporting to work the first day at Brown Express. (Labor unions were strong in those days, and the pay I received was very good.)

About one month before graduation, I had landed a job assisting in emphysema research at Southwestern Medical School in Dallas. My boss, Dr. Johansen, was understanding enough to allow me to leave work thirty minutes early so that I could make the fifteen-minute drive to the freight dock at Brown Express. There I would quickly change clothes in my car and report to work at the dock at 5:00 p.m.

At this second job, I worked until 10:30 or 11:00 o'clock at night. Both jobs were Monday through Friday. At the freight dock I also worked most Saturdays.

Debbie didn't work outside the house most of this time. Due to my heavy work load we didn't see much of each other except on weekends. During this period our marriage began to break down. I took a while to catch on to what was happening, due partially to the fact that I was gone so much. I loved Debbie and our son Brian dearly, and I tried desperately to save the marriage. I don't blame Debbie, for she was still a teenager when we were married, and she probably felt she hadn't yet experienced enough of life to be tied down with a family. The more the marriage began to unravel, the more I tried to hold it together.

In previous years of extreme mental illness, I had often surmised that I would never marry because I assumed my mental problems meant I could never be a fit husband or father. This had saddened me greatly for years. When Debbie and I did get married and then had a child, I felt that a dream had come true! I couldn't believe that I was really a husband and father. I think it might have been this unbridled joy and feeling of fulfillment that led to a partial remission of my OCD during our first three years of marriage and that allowed me to graduate from college and work for a while at two jobs.

I had thought for many years that I probably *shouldn't* ever have children, so great was my fear that they too would be afflicted with my *insanity* and destined to lives of torment. Before our son Brian was born and while he was an infant, my habit was to pray hard every night and to plead with God that Brian not be afflicted with mental illness. Thank the Lord, my fears never became a reality.

When the marriage began to go on the rocks, my obsessive-compulsive disorder returned with a vengeance. OCD became so bad that I was forced to resign from my job at the medical school after working there for a year. I lied to Debbie. I told her that I was resigning because I could make more money working exclusively at the freight dock.

In the meantime, Debbie had obtained a job at a nearby pharmacy. Soon afterward, she told me that she no longer loved me and that she had to move on. With OCD now controlling my life, I felt as if my wife and child were the only things I had to live for. Now those things were being taken from me. My outlook on life became very bleak.

9 COMMON HORSE SENSE

Debbie never knew that I suffered from mental illness. She probably noticed, however, that I displayed strange and erratic behaviors at times. To Debbie my erratic behavior translated into a lack of common sense. "Reagan is book smart, but hasn't got any common sense," Debbie was fond of saying. I didn't care if she felt this way, just as long as my secret illness wasn't discovered.

I really can't fault Debbie or anyone else for believing this because my behavior was certainly bizarre at times. Debbie knew that I wanted to become an optometrist. I had applied and been accepted to the University of Houston College of Optometry. My real dream had been to become a physician, but OCD had been responsible for wrecking my college grades during my junior year. I didn't even bother to apply to medical school knowing that, on the basis of those grades, I wouldn't have a chance of being accepted. Even with crippling OCD at times during high school, I had graduated with a 90 average, but my illness, especially while I was a junior in college, destroyed my chances of becoming a medical doctor.

One of the primary reasons I had wanted to become a physician was the possibility that I could heal myself of my mental illness without anyone else's finding out about my secret ailment.

Debbie probably considered me whimsical because of my decision not to go to optometry school. What she couldn't have known about was the terrible panic attack in Houston when we had traveled there to check out the optometry school. She was also unaware of the horrible conflict which arose in my mind when I learned that a pair of glasses can contain two different strength lenses. (These items will be discussed in a later chapter.)

Some of my acquaintances also thought I lacked common sense. The last job I held while Debbie and I were married was the part-time job at the freight docks. Why would a man with a college degree settle for a part-time job loading and unloading freight?

I'm sure Debbie would have divorced me anyway, but had I not been mentally ill, I could probably have attended medical school, dental school, or optometry school without her.

I did many things that indicated that I was lacking in common sense. One example was the occasion when I purchased the color television, then decided to return it. I did dozens of "strange things" while married to Debbie. I do not find it surprising that she and some of our friends felt that I was seriously deficient in the common-sense category. That was fine with me. I had them all fooled! They had no idea that I was mentally ill.

There were numerous occasions when I was so preoccupied with obsessive-compulsive thoughts that I did not think problems and situations through thoroughly. As a result, I made bad decisions that led others to conclude that I didn't possess good common horse sense.

10 THE COLOR ORANGE

Months before my marriage ended, I was finding it increasingly difficult to work at even one job. OCD was running so rampantly in my life that concentrating on work at the freight dock became exceedingly arduous.

The roof of the dock was held up by huge steel girders. One night while unloading freight from a trailer, I noticed a large rusty nail lying at the base of one of the girders. I thought, "That nail shouldn't be lying there. It should be thrown in a trash barrel and gotten rid of."

My job was just to unload freight, so I continued working. But I couldn't get the nail out of my thoughts. I kept thinking and thinking about it. For many nights on the dock, I found the nail continuously on my mind. How I would like to throw it away! But I could not let myself. I didn't want to succumb to what I thought was an aberrant impulse.

After a few days had elapsed, whenever I would work in the vicinity of the place the nail had been, I wouldn't let myself look to see if it was still there at the base of that girder. I guess I didn't want the mental image of the nail to get any clearer in my mind because I feared the agony might accelerate.

The thought of the nail tormented me for months. The abnormal mental mechanism at work concerning the obsession with the rusty nail may have also contributed to the spawning of the following events.

I had stopped smoking cigarettes and had substituted gum chewing. There was a gumball machine on the dock, and each night I would buy several gumballs.

One night I put a nickel in the machine, and out rolled an orange gumball. I considered this odd because I couldn't remember ever having gotten an orange one before, and I had chewed many dozens over the months. I put it into my mouth and began to chew. I couldn't stop thinking about how uncommon it was to get an orange gumball. This gumball seemed a freak. I began to feel uncomfortable with it. But the feeling was silly. Nothing was wrong with an orange gumball, I told myself.

I felt more and more uneasy. The more anxious I became, the more uncomfortable I felt with the gumball. All this time I was unloading freight from a forty-five foot trailer. I tried to lose myself in my work and, by doing so, to forget the orange gumball.

It wasn't the entire gumball which was bothering me--just the fact that it was orange. But there was nothing wrong with *orange*, was there? The only problem was that an orange gumball had never before rolled out of the machine for me. "What exactly is it you are worried about?" I asked myself. I couldn't answer that question. Then I began thinking that maybe, if I bought another gumball and if it wasn't orange, but one of the ordinary colors which was usually dispensed into my hand from the machine, I wouldn't have to worry about the orange one. My mind began telling me that, if I bought a gumball of another color, it would cancel out the *freak orange gumball.* The only problem was that, if I gave in to the obsession-compulsion, I would feel defeated. I was in a lose/lose situation.

About two hours had elapsed since I had purchased the orange gumball, and the obsessional conflict in my mind was becoming so enormously powerful that I was having difficulty concentrating on doing my job. I was becoming very anxious. My mind was at war with itself! One side wanted to resist buying another gumball and thereby not give in to the terrible, hideous obsession. The other side wanted desperately to buy another gumball in order to "cancel out" the orange one.

The "other side" won the battle. I rushed up to the gumball machine, thrust in another nickel, and held my breath as I turned the knob, hoping against hope that the new gumball would be some color other than the dreaded "orange."

It wasn't orange! I pushed it into my mouth and started chewing. But the victory was hollow. I had surrendered to an enemy impulse which I didn't understand. I was terrified! Impulses were controlling my very existence!

The price I paid for this surrender was dear. For the next ten years I tried at every opportunity to avoid everything orange. Orange objects made me feel intensely uncomfortable. I stopped wearing any orange article of clothing. I wouldn't buy anything that was colored orange. The University of Syracuse Orangemen football team was a team I would not watch on television, although I loved to watch football.

Later, when my second wife Marsha and I had only been dating a couple of months, she phoned to tell me that her brother Don had helped her buy a new car. I excitedly asked her to describe it, and she told me that it was a Chevrolet Camero with bucket seats, automatic transmission, V-8 engine, etc. I was overjoyed! I didn't have a car at the time, but now that my girlfriend had a new car, I couldn't have been happier. I asked her what color it was. She replied, "Orange."

I gasped, "Orange! Why did you get orange?" I was shocked and appalled! But what was I to say? I couldn't tell my new girlfriend that I was intensely uncomfortable with anything orange. If I did, she might abruptly become my ex-girlfriend!

I had been very happy moments before this news; now I was extremely distressed. Marsha asked, "Would you like me to drive it over to your apartment?"

I stammered, "Yes."

She arrived in her new car about an hour later. We went for a ride. I was very uncomfortable the whole time.

In the ensuing months I was to ride in that car many times, and, in retrospect, I see that the orange car may have turned out to be good therapy for my irrational phobia because it forced me to deal with the color, instead of running away from it.

About two years later, after our marriage, my wife Marsha and I were given an orange stroller as a baby-shower gift for our first born. I begged Marsha to take it back. She refused, reminding me that the gift was from her sister and saying that it would be rude and ridiculous to return it.

So strong was my aversion to that particular color that ten years passed before I would so much as eat an orange or drink orange juice.

Why did I develop a phobia for the color "orange"? The answer to this riddle remained a mystery to me for almost two decades. I believe I now have the answer.

During that particular period in my life, my marriage to Debbie had been rapidly breaking apart, and the resultant stress and anxiety, for some mysterious reason, found a *home* in the color "orange." Some individuals get migraine headaches or ulcers as a result of stress. I developed a phobia.

If a doctor had informed me at the time that stress over a crumbling marriage had made me afraid of orange, I probably wouldn't have believed it, or, at best, I would have found it farfetched.

I have come to realize, however, some things that I didn't comprehend then. The human mind is a wonderful, powerful, often puzzling and eerily mysterious entity. Scientists are just beginning to understand the workings of the mind. For many, many years the workings of my mind were totally unexplainable and baffling. I am now comforted because I understand more of why my mind, for such a long time, seemed to operate so irrationally.

11 TO THE DOCTOR

My divorce from Debbie became final on November 30, 1971. My four-year-old son Brian meant the world to me. Now I had lost both him and Debbie! I thought I had nothing to live for. The stress created by my deteriorating marriage had brought my OCD to a peak. Though still employed part time at the freight dock, I had become so emotionally disturbed and preoccupied that it was impossible for me to work much. Every time I tried, I became extremely obsessed with crazy thoughts that made my work a living hell.

I was living in the apartment that Debbie and I had shared. I drank heavily each day to try to ease the OCD symptoms and to alleviate my depression. Little did I know that in less than two months I would meet the love of my life, Marsha. I will always believe that the Good Lord brought us together.

I had never seen a doctor regarding my mental illness nor gotten any medicine with which to treat it.

One day, in desperation, I asked my sister to drive me over to her doctor's office. She did. I went in to see Dr. Sikora, a family practitioner, to ask him to give me a prescription for tranquilizers to calm me. I was afraid to tell him much, and I didn't. He stood there and talked with me for a few minutes, and he apparently realized that there was a much deeper problem present than I was relating. He inquired, "Is your sister with you?" I reluctantly replied that she was in her car in the parking lot. He stated, "I would like to speak with her."

Dr. Sikora then led the way to the parking lot where he confronted Sheila. "Your brother is a very sick young man," he said, "and I urge you to convince him to see a psychiatrist."

I was aware that spilling my long-held secret to a psychiatrist might mean a trip to a mental hospital for me. But I had to take the risk. I was weary of running away from the problem. I had run from it for twenty years. If I was to survive, I had to get a grip on myself and take some positive action toward getting help for myself.

I reluctantly took Dr. Sikora's advice. At his suggestion, I drove over to the Southern Methodist University campus and talked to a counselor at the huge Methodist church there. The counselor recommended three psychiatrists. I selected one of them. That's how I met Dr. Samuel Neely, my first psychiatrist.

I called Dr. Neely and scheduled an appointment. The day of the appointment I caught a city bus to his north-Dallas office. I walked into the building and up a flight of stairs. When I reached my hand out for the door knob, I couldn't make myself open the door! For twenty years I had been fighting mental illness without anyone's knowing it but myself. What would be the consequences if I told someone else of my dark secret? I turned around and briskly ran back down the stairs and out of the building. Then I stopped! Could I live in fear the rest of my life? What kind of life was this? I was weary. I felt my life was going to end if I didn't act. I had come to the end of the line. I turned, walked back up the stairs, and entered Dr. Neely's waiting room.

Soon the doctor came out and beckoned me into his office. He had a black beard of medium length and looked very much like the caricatures of psychiatrists. I sat down on a couch and, with great trepidation, told Dr. Neely of my illness. When I finished, I thought he might pick up the phone and call the State Mental Hospital in Terrel, Texas, to come and get me. Instead, to my great relief, he said he was going to try to help me! He scheduled another appointment, and I began seeing him regularly twice a week. He prescribed Valium for me, and over the next few weeks, I slowly began to improve.

12 THE PANIC ATTACKS

Over the years I've experienced three major panic attacks. These attacks occurred during a nine-year period. The first happened in high school.

I had attended a dance at my high school one night during my sophomore year. After dancing a few times with different girls, I was asked by a senior named Bob to step out behind the building and smoke a cigarette with him. I replied, "Sure," and we went outside together. He reached into his pocket, pulled out a pack of cigarettes, and handed me one. I had never smoked a whole cigarette before, but I took it and lit up as if it were a daily occurrence. We stood there talking and puffing for several minutes. I felt very mature.

The following day was Saturday. About three o'clock in the afternoon, my father was working somewhere on our farm, and my mother was sewing in my sister's bedroom. I was walking through the house when suddenly something hit me like a lightning bolt from the blue. I was suddenly terrified! And there was no apparent reason. I ran as fast as my legs would carry me into my parents' bedroom and flailed myself face down upon their bed. My mind felt as if it were exploding into a thousand pieces. My mind and body seemed to be coming unraveled. It seemed I was in a state of total insanity! My heart was pounding like a bass drum. I thrashed around on the bed for minutes that seemed like hours. (This was the indescribable fright that I imagine one might experience if he were looking out the window to see a tornado 100 yards away and approaching rapidly! But there was no tornado.) There was nothing to be afraid of. The fear seemed to come out of nowhere. But this fear was all consuming. Every fiber of my body shook with panic.

After what seemed an eternity, my body and mind slowly began to recover and relax. Gradually I returned to sanity. I had experienced my first full-blown panic attack. Upon regaining my composure, I walked out of the bedroom trying to act as if nothing had happened. For over ten years I didn't breathe a word to anyone of what had occurred.

I can only guess about what precipitated this attack. It might have been guilt spawned by the smoking of the cigarette the previous night. Or maybe OCD-related anxiety had been building for quite some time and required release.

The second attack came after I had completed college and worked at Southwestern Medical School for one year. I had applied and been accepted to the University of Houston College of Optometry. Debbie and I drove to Houston one weekend shortly after my acceptance to tour the optometry school. My aunt Ava lived in Houston. Upon entering the city, I stopped at a phone booth, opened the phone directory, and begin searching for her number. Then panic struck again! I stood in the phone booth trembling. My hands shook. My body shook. I endured the suffering in the booth until the attack finally began to subside. I regained enough control to search again for Ava's number and dial it. When Aunt Ava answered, I told her that we were in town and would like to come by for a visit. It required every fiber of my strength to attempt to sound normal.

On the way to her house, I stopped at a convenience store, purchased a tin of aspirin, and gobbled down three of them, hoping they would help me relax. This incident occurred at least two years before I received any medication for anxiety. I told Debbie that the aspirins were for a headache.

Upon reaching Ava's house, I rang the doorbell; we were invited in and sat down to chat. I hoped and prayed that no one would notice my shaky body and quivering voice. I must have put on a fine performance because no one appeared to notice. I had become a master at cover-up.

While visiting Ava, I experienced something else significant. Ava stated, "So, Reagan, you're going to become an eye doctor. Let me show you my glasses prescription that my doctor wrote for me just this morning."

She handed me the prescription. I looked it over. Something about it suddenly blew my mind! The eye doctor had prescribed two different strength lenses, one strength for each eye. I had never worn eyeglasses or visited an eye doctor. I didn't know that a person's eyes could be different. I wanted everything to be perfect, equal, symmetrical. I quickly came to the conclusion that I could never become an optometrist. I could never prescribe different strength lenses to a person!

A month later I wrote to the optometry school saying I wouldn't be attending in the fall due to financial problems. I lied. Only I knew the real reason I couldn't become an optometrist. My heart ached as I gave up my dream of becoming an eye doctor. In my mind I had no other choice!

The third attack came a couple of weeks before my divorce from Debbie was final. I had invited to my apartment the nineteen-year-old girl who lived next door. The only thing we did all night was talk. I liked her. It appeared she liked me. She asked if I would take her to work the next afternoon, and I agreed. I was to knock on her door at 3:45 p.m. and drive her to the drugstore where she was employed.

At approximately 2:00 p.m. that afternoon I experienced my third panic attack. I became so distraught that I forgot to meet the girl at the proper time. Suddenly there was a knock upon my door. It was the girl. She declared, “I thought that you were to give me a ride to work.”

I stammered, “Of course, I'm just running late.” I lied. I always lied to prevent my being found out. No one could know I was mentally ill.

I drove the girl to work, but I don't think I said more than two words to her the whole journey. I'm sure she wondered what was wrong with me since we had had such a delightful evening the night before. She never had anything to do with me after that episode.

I now believe that the panic attacks were triggered by the same anxiety which activated my obsessive-compulsive disorder. I have discussed this presumption with my doctor, and he tends to concur.

13 THE ABYSS

On January 20, 1972, I was at my sister Sheila's house in north Dallas. She told me that a mutual friend had called and asked if I would consider having a blind date. My first reaction was to decline. Later that day I reconsidered and accepted the date.

That's how I met Marsha. We had our first date on January 21, 1972. I liked her instantly! She was attractive and intelligent. We began dating every week.

I moved into an apartment with a college buddy named Ted, who was attending Baylor College of Dentistry in Dallas. I still wasn't able to work. I had lost my wife and son, but now things were looking up because I had a girlfriend whom I cared for and who cared for me.

Late one Friday afternoon the following April, I called Marsha and asked her out. She explained, "I can't go out with you tonight, Reagan, because I already have a date."

I was stunned. I begged her to break it and go out with me instead! She refused. She told me she would consider going out with me on Saturday night. To me that was unacceptable. I believed that, if Marsha went out with this other man, she might become attached to him, and our relationship would be over. I became horrified! I was about to lose my girlfriend, the last thing in the world I wanted to lose. I would be left with nothing: no girlfriend, no wife, no son, no job.

Ted was in his bedroom studying that night. I was sitting on the couch listening to sad music and feeling very sorry for myself. I reached into my pocket and pulled out my recently refilled prescription of Valium. I set the bottle on the coffee table and stared at it for what seemed a long time. I located a piece of paper and a pen and wrote a suicide note. In the note, I asked God to forgive me for what I was about to do.

I poured the Valium tablets out on top of the coffee table. Then I counted them. There were ninety-two pills. I began to swallow them. I swallowed all ninety-two tablets. I was heartbroken and angry, and I wanted Marsha to become aware of my anguish. I telephoned her and told her of what I had done. She told me to call an ambulance immediately! I refused and hung up. Minutes later the phone began ringing, but I wouldn't answer it. It rang and rang. Ted came out of his bedroom and answered. It was my sister's husband, Ike. Marsha had called him, and now he was telling Ted what I had done.

Ted screamed, "Come on, Reagan, get into my car and let's rush to the hospital!" I stubbornly refused. Ted begged. He pleaded, but to no avail. Then, in desperation, Ted phoned the police.

Moments later there came a knock at the door. Ted opened it, and four Dallas police officers stormed into the room. By this time I was feeling very groggy. The police officers lifted me onto a stretcher, and I was carried out the door and down the steps, where I was loaded into a waiting ambulance. I was rushed to Parkland Hospital. At Parkland, I was given a liquid to drink; I started vomiting. I heaved and vomited for about fifteen minutes. Then I was taken to a room for observation.

Later that night, I opened my eyes, and Ted was entering the room. We spoke to each other. He asked, "How are you feeling?"

I replied that I was feeling well.

I can still visualize his face that night. It was very thoughtful of him to drive over to visit me, since Parkland Hospital was a considerable distance from his apartment.

The next morning, before being dismissed, I had to speak with a hospital psychiatrist. He called Dr. Neely and informed him of the incident.

I caught a bus back to the apartment. Ted was there. I told him how considerate he had been to visit me in the middle of the night. He replied, “Reagan, I didn't visit you.”

I replied, “Come on, Ted, you're joking.”

He exclaimed, “I swear I didn't go to the hospital last night!”

I was speechless! To this day I can still picture his face in my hospital room. I later talked to Dr. Neely about this, and he said I had experienced a hallucination!

A couple of days later Ted notified me that the apartment manager was insisting that I move out. I went to talk to her and pleaded with her to let me stay, but it was no use. She was adamant. She was evicting me.

Marsha and I got back together, and she helped me find a place to live. We didn't discuss my attempted suicide for at least fifteen years.

14 SAVED BY GRACE

When Marsha and I had been dating for about a year, I was living in a two-room apartment in Irving, about a mile from her house.

At the time I was experiencing hell on earth. OCD and depression were so severe and debilitating that I could barely function. Marsha was working full time at a department store, and she wasn't fully aware of the torturous existence that I was living from day to day.

I was too sick to work and drew unemployment benefits for a few months. Daddy had helped me with a down payment on a new Chevrolet Vega, but I was having trouble making the monthly payments. Marsha was helping me at times with my car payments. My self esteem was at an all-time low. I had been fighting mental illness for 20 years, and I was losing the battle!

After I had attempted suicide by swallowing the Valium tablets, Dr. Neely, at my request, had changed my medication to Phenobarbital. I could no longer afford Valium which cost about $100 a bottle. In contrast, Phenobarbital was inexpensive. At the time he prescribed it, Dr. Neely cautioned me that Phenobarbital was a much deadlier medication when it came to overdosing and that, unlike Valium, Phenobarbital could kill a person in a hurry.

I again had lost the desire to live. My life had become constant misery. Late one night I decided to end it all. I had in my pocket an almost full bottle of Phenobarbital. I knew that would do the trick. I just wanted relief from the living hell that I was experiencing.

I had nothing to look forward to--no career, no wife, no family. Nothing! I couldn't expect Marsha to continue dating me or to marry me and support me for the rest of my life. She had already been helping support me for several months. This wasn't fair to her. No one would want to be married to an emotional cripple. She was all I had, but it seemed I really didn't have her.

When I had overdosed on Valium at Ted's apartment, I really hadn't wanted to kill myself. I know this sounds bizarre, but my main motivation for taking the Valium was a type of twisted revenge. I had wanted to strike back at Marsha for going out with another man. I also had been wallowing in self pity. Deep down in my heart though, I really hadn't wanted to die.

This was different. This time I was going to end it all. No more games--this was the real thing!

I drove down the street leading to the two-room apartment, where I had spent most of my hours in wasted, useless living; actually "existing" was a more appropriate term than "living." My thoughts were so twisted that I was weary of trying to continue to make sense of anything. Life no longer had any meaning. All was useless. All was futile.

I pulled my car into the driveway, walked to my apartment, and unlocked the door. I entered the darkened room. All the windows had dark curtains covering them, and even during the day, it was one of the dreariest rooms I have ever encountered.

I sat down on the bed, took the bottle of Phenobarbital out of my pocket, and laid it beside me. For minutes that seemed like hours, I sat there contemplating killing myself.

The hour was late. I looked at my watch. The time was 1:30 a.m. If I was going to do it, I was going to do it now.

Suddenly, an unbidden thought entered my mind. I thought of calling Bill Hanshaw, a friend of the family who had dated my sister off and on for years. About three years ago, my first wife and I had visited Bill at his home in Dallas. He had been raised a Methodist by Christian parents who were close friends of my parents.

Suddenly I wanted to call Bill. It was past 2:00 a.m., and he lived on the opposite side of Dallas. That really didn't matter. I was desperate. Since I had no phone, I got into my car, drove one block to a convenience store with a phone booth, and called Bill.

Bill answered the phone. I can't remember what exactly I said to him, but it must have sounded urgent because he said, "Don't do anything! Tell me where you are, and I'll be there as quickly as possible."

When Bill drove up, I was waiting in the driveway of my apartment. We walked to my room and entered.

I told Bill everything. He listened and heard it all. Then he began talking about the Lord and what the Lord had done for him. I had become detached from the Lord over the last few years, but I listened intently and heard every word.

(I had always respected Bill Hanshaw. Upon graduating from high school in my hometown of Raymondville, he had received an appointment to West Point. He later graduated with a degree in architecture from the University of Texas in Austin. Bill had for a time worked at NASA and had helped design one of the instruments used by astronauts on the moon.)

The things he said to me that night sounded good--sounded encouraging. My faith in the Lord had diminished in recent years, and I asked Bill, "How can a person with your intellect be so believing and trusting in God?"

He replied, "Reagan, I stopped trying to force faith through my head, and instead I let it enter through my heart!"

I'll never forget those words! Before he left my apartment, Bill said a prayer for me, then handed me a copy of the Gospel of St. John.

On that dark, gloomy night in Irving, Bill Hanshaw saved my life!

15 PHOBIAS AND THE MENTAL WARD

I continued to be severely mentally disturbed. The date was in late 1972. Irrational phobias were now controlling my life. I hadn't been to see Dr. Neely in a long time because I lacked money. The Phenobarbital I was taking wasn't helping.

I had decided I wanted to marry Marsha even if I was mentally ill and didn't have a job.

After much mental torment, I decided that a getaway would be good for me. I thought that maybe, if I got away from Irving for a while, I would be able to sort things out and perhaps ease my troubled mind.

I traveled to the Rio Grande Valley in South Texas to visit my parents. I thought that maybe I would be helped if I discussed my symptoms with my mother.

This was a time when phobias were really beginning to take hold in my life. Besides the color *orange,* I became afraid of the letter *f*. I don't know exactly why, but I know this phobia was related to *f* 's being the first letter of the four-letter "*f*-word." In my distorted thinking, I became fearful of anything that began with the letter *f*, even such words as *flowers*.

Many sofas and stuffed chairs have *f*loral designs on them. I would not sit on a chair or sofa if it had a *f*loral design. To do so would create immediate anxiety in me, and I would become extremely uncomfortable. My mother had put *f*loral patterned sheets on my bed; they fostered anxiety and caused me to have trouble sleeping.

One night I stayed up late with my mother and told her some of my phobia symptoms concerning *orange* and the letter *f*. I also told her of my fear of the number *13* and of the subsequent and related fear of the letter *m*.

After I realized that *m* was the 13th letter of the alphabet, I became disturbed by the name *M*arsha because it begins with an *m*. I became concerned that this revelation might destroy our relationship, that because of my fear I might not be able to feel comfortable with her again because her name began with the 13th letter of the alphabet!

One day I realized that my father's name, M.C., also began with *m*. This recognition comforted me because, for some neurotic reason, since my father's name started with that letter, it suddenly became *all right* to love a girl whose first name began with *m*.

I also informed Mama of my perfectionist handwriting obsession, my wanting all the letters to be perfect.

I had never before confided any of my neurotic thoughts or feelings to my mother. When I was through, she acted as if she understood and gave me some advice. She said that the next morning I should sit down at their table and start writing to try to get over my handwriting problem.

The next morning I sat down at the kitchen table and began copying an article from the newspaper.

About an hour later the doorbell rang. The person at the door was my uncle Raymond. He was invited in, and we stood there talking. Suddenly, there was another ring of the doorbell. There stood Talmadge Mayo, a dear friend of my parents.

I began to feel that there was something peculiar about this situation. Then Mama informed me that the three of them were going to take me to the mental hospital in Harlingen.

I was horrified! But what could I do? How could I fight Raymond, Talmadge, and Mama? Raymond is an average-sized man. Talmadge is a huge man about 6' 2" and 225 pounds and as strong as an ox. Physically I was not their equal. And they were family; they were friends. I could not fight them.

So I went with them to the mental hospital. The day was Saturday. I was interviewed by a nurse and afterward was informed that the hospital did not admit patients on the weekend.

My mother became very upset, but after some lengthy debate she finally realized that there was nothing she could do but bring me back to the hospital the following Monday. To my great relief, we all went back home.

I was horrified by the thought of being *caged up* in a mental ward! I wanted to escape.

I had no money for gasoline, or so I initially thought. Then I remembered a check for $20 that my father had given me earlier. (Daddy slipped me a little money from time to time when I was with him.) I had put the check into my billfold, and now I frantically searched for it. I found it!

I formulated a devious little plan to get away from the Valley before I was committed to the hospital.

The evening of the next day, Sunday, I told my mother that I was going into Raymondville to purchase a six-pack of beer. My parents were against the drinking of alcoholic beverages; therefore, I reasoned that if I confided in my mother that I was going to buy beer, she would believe me.

The plan worked! She believed me! I got into my car and drove into Raymondville to a convenience store, where I cashed my $20 check. I filled my car with gas and headed for Dallas. I arrived in Dallas eight hours later and then drove to my apartment in Irving.

I was miserable! I was mentally sick and miserable! I entered my two-room apartment and flopped down on my bed. I thought the end of the world had come for me. I was very ill. Experts had told me that hospitalization wouldn't help. I couldn't afford a psychiatrist or proper medication. All seemed hopeless!

Then there was a knock at my door. I opened the door, and there stood Marsha. I invited her into my apartment. I was very glad to see her! We sat on my bed, and I poured out my heart to her.

I told her how distressed I was, and what *they* had tried to do to me. I told her how *they* had tried to get me committed to a mental hospital.

I now realize that my mother, Raymond, and Talmadge had nothing but the best intentions and that they were desperately trying to help me. But at the time this message didn't seem clear.

Marsha was the most understanding and compassionate person there could have been at that moment. I will never forget that moment, and I shall be eternally grateful to her for being there by my side during this painful ordeal!

16 THE KNIFE

Probably my most horrifying and frightening obsession was the knife obsession. This obsession occurred in 1972 after Marsha and I had been dating for several months.

Occasionally we would sunbathe in her mother's backyard. Once while in the backyard joyfully soaking up the sun's rays, I felt a ghastly thought cross my mind: "What if I got a knife and stabbed Marsha?"

I tried to shake the thought, but it wouldn't shake! I kept on thinking it repeatedly, like a record player that's stuck on a single groove! The more I thought it, the more anxious I became. The more anxious I became, the more powerful the obsession became. It was a vicious circle!

For the next few days, anytime I would be with Marsha, the knife obsession would also be there.

I hadn't seen Dr. Neely for approximately a year, mainly due to lack of money, but this obsession was so scary that I booked an appointment with him immediately. This obsession couldn't wait!

The knife obsession was one of the worst obsessions that ever troubled me because it concerned a person whom I loved dearly and it was about hurting her. I was scared! I was very scared! I couldn't understand why I would have horrible thoughts like these!

I walked into Dr. Neely's office, sat down on a couch, and told him about my terrible dilemma. I stated, in an unsteady voice: "Dr. Neely, I've been thinking about stabbing Marsha with a knife, and I can't get this thought out of my mind. It's driving me crazy!"

The doctor peered over at me, and I wondered, "Is he going to call the 'Funny Farm' right now and tell them to come and get me?"

Dr. Neely looked me straight in the eye and solemnly questioned: "Are you going to use a knife with a short blade or one with a long blade?"

At first I stared at him dumbfounded! Then I began to laugh. Dr. Neely also began to laugh. We sat there and laughed and laughed.

That unexpected comment was probably the best thing he could have said to me because it released all the tension from my body and defused the issue.

This episode illustrates how, while words can be powerful negative forces, they can also be potent positive ones.

Dr. Neely looked at me and declared, "You're mad at her!"

I questioned, "Oh, really?"

He continued, "Yes, you're angry with Marsha, and you're not showing it. You're not showing your feelings. This is one of the main problems concerning your illness; you don't show your feelings. You're keeping them all bottled up inside. You're angry at Marsha right now for some reason, and you're keeping the anger bottled up. You're not admitting to yourself or to Marsha that you're angry with her."

* * *

After all these years, I believe that one reason I may have been angry with Marsha was that, in my mind, I felt that she was pressuring me to marry her. I did want to marry her; at least most of me did. I had asked her to marry me on several occasions.

However, I was very leery of marriage, especially after my bad experience with it. My first marriage had ended in disaster! I feared making the same mistake.

An accompanying problem concerned the date on which we were planning to be married. I kept changing the date.

The first date we set was April 1. Then I decided that we couldn't be married on that day because it's April Fool's Day.

Subsequently, at my suggestion, we picked April 21. I thought I could be comfortable with this date because I had been married to my first wife on April 21. But then I remembered that that marriage failed! So April 21 was out of the question.

We then picked May 8. My troubled and irrational mind couldn't initially find anything wrong with May 8. Then this thought occurred to me: if you turn the numeral 8 on its side, it becomes the symbol for *infinity*. *Infinity* was one of my *bad words* (I'll explain further in a later chapter). So I couldn't be wed on the 8th either.

It was then that Marsha put her foot down and stated that, if I was ever going to marry her, it had to be on May 8. She was not going to allow me to change the date again.

I relented. I now believe that all the date changing was related to my anxiety concerning remarriage.

I was extremely nervous, but we were married on May 8. That was one of the best decisions of my life!

* * *

Now, back to the knife obsession--Dr. Neely harshly stated: "Reagan, you've got to start showing your feelings!"

That statement was a warning! He gave me a book called *The Angry Book;* I took it home and read it. After reading the book I could understand what he meant about my bottling up my feelings.

This session with Dr. Neely was just one isolated session, but it worked wonders. Within a few days, I forgot the knife fixation. It was gone, never to return. That one session of psychotherapy with Dr. Neely rid me of that horrifying obsession.

As time passed, I learned to express my feelings more freely.

17 MARSHA AND I GET MARRIED

Marsha and I were married secretly on May 8, 1973. We had driven to the federal courthouse in downtown Dallas. When we entered the building, I immediately got cold feet and insisted on returning to the car. There I consumed a quart of beer and, subsequently, felt ready for matrimony.

We entered a courtroom and met the judge who was to perform the ceremony. The justice was amused by the fact that both Marsha and I were Smiths, as was our witness. After we tied the knot, we kept our marriage secret.

One evening a few days later, I went over to Sharon's apartment. (Sharon was one of Marsha's older sisters who, like everyone else, knew nothing of the marriage.) I consumed a few mixed drinks and began to cry. I told Sharon that Marsha and I were married and that I wasn't sure how much I loved Marsha. Sharon tried to console me, and she asked me to stay the night in the guest bedroom.

The next day I drove back to my apartment. Meanwhile, Sharon and her husband Conrad drove to Marsha's mother's house and told the family about the wedding.

The same night, Marsha's older brother Don, accompanied by Conrad, paid me a visit at my apartment. Don was 19 years older than Marsha and 15 years my senior.

Don asked me if it was true that Marsha and I had been married. I replied affirmatively. He then asked if I had told Sharon that I didn't know how much I loved Marsha.

I answered, "Yes, I said that."

"You, son-of-a-bitch," Don bellowed. "I'm going to have the marriage annulled!"

"No!" I shouted.

"What?" Don asked. "You don't want the marriage annulled?"

"No, I don't!" I insisted.

Don seemed perplexed by the inconsistencies of my statements.

On the one hand, I admitted that I had told Sharon that I didn't know how much I loved Marsha. But on the other hand, I was emphatically insisting that I didn't want the marriage terminated.

At that time, Don, I believe, determined that I needed help. "I'm going to take you to the mental hospital in Terrel. I want you to admit yourself," Don stated.

He recognized a problem because Don himself had a close friend who at times became mentally unstable. This friend had been helped on a few occasions at the hospital in Terrel.

"A hospital probably won't help me," I said. "My psychiatrist, Dr. Neely, told me that I couldn't receive much help in a mental hospital. Let me strike a deal with you," I continued. "I'll call another psychiatrist and ask him if a mental hospital will help a person with my type of problem. I'll go willingly to Terrel if the doctor says that the hospital will benefit me. But if he says a hospital won't help me, then let's try a different approach." Don agreed to the deal.

The next morning I called a psychiatrist and put the question to him. He answered, "Unfortunately, mental hospitals are largely ineffective in treating OCD patients."

I informed Don of what the doctor had said. He declared, "OK, Reagan, I won't take you to the hospital, but

I will demand that you come out of your shell and move into the house with Marsha and start learning to live a more normal life. I want you to start joining the family in going to some movies and restaurants occasionally.

"You have been holed up in your apartment for weeks, not coming into contact with the outside world. These are my requirements," Don stated.

I agreed to do as my new brother-in-law asked. I moved out of my apartment and into Marsha's house. I began working with Don and his friend Gary in the siding business.

My frame of mind began gradually to improve.

18 THE WALLS

Marsha and I traveled to the Rio Grande Valley in South Texas and moved into an apartment in Raymondville in the autumn of 1973. I quickly landed a job at the sugar mill just outside the small town of Santa Rosa, approximately 20 miles from Raymondville.

OCD was again giving me problems, and I was drinking too much. Marsha told me I should drink less, but my standard reply was, "Marsha, I would rather be an alcoholic than be neurotic." When I drank, the alcohol in my system reduced the OCD symptoms. But now, the alcohol was creating problems of its own.

I worked eight-hour shifts at the sugar mill. After two weeks everyone rotated to a new shift, usually with no days off. The constant rotating was stressful to me. The biggest stress producer wasn't the changing shifts, however. The biggest stress producer was my supervisor, a young 23-year-old man named Joe.

I loved the job at the sugar mill, and to this day I believe I did a good job. But Joe was constantly critical.

I worked in the water-treatment department. One of my co-workers was Ben, who held a college degree in chemistry and knew more about the water department than Joe did. Ben ran the department until he was moved into the lab as a bench chemist.

Ben and I got along well, but after he departed, Joe took charge and immediately began acting like a tyrant. Nothing I did pleased him. He was constantly faultfinding. The job at the sugar mill was adding stress to my life, and my OCD was getting worse.

* * *

One Saturday when I wasn't working, I invited five friends to our apartment for a poker game. Only one person came to play. It was Tommy, a dear friend of mine.

I felt rejected and hurt that no one else came to play poker, and I began to drink beer. When it became obvious that no one else was coming, I drank more and more. Then I began to telephone those people who were missing.

I remember that I called Bob and practically begged him to come. Tommy was sitting across from me shaking his head and trying to dissuade me from making a fool of myself.

I hung up the phone and began to cry. I sat there in the kitchen and sobbed in front of Tommy, telling him how embarrassed I was that no one else had come. After a while Tommy went home.

Suddenly I became furious because only one individual had come to play poker. I went into a rage! I doubled my fist and pounded the wall! My fist went right through the wall and left a sizable hole. I was shocked. Then I struck the wall again and again, creating a larger and larger hole.

I had lost control. I knew a little karate from my days in Dallas when I had earned a green belt, so I began kicking the walls, opening up huge holes in the sheetrock. I charged around the living room kicking in walls. I was leaving gaping holes three and four feet in diameter.

Marsha was horrified! She tried to stop me. I wouldn't stop until our living room was in shambles! Finally, I lay down on the couch and passed out.

Marsha was already awake when I arose the following morning. She walked into the living room, inspected the damage, and glared at me.

"I hope you're proud of yourself!" she screeched. "You've really done it now."

I stared at her, then I gazed around the room at the wreckage. I spotted a piece of sheetrock that extended into one of the holes I had created. I roared, "Here's a place I missed," and I abruptly kicked that sheetrock in also. Marsha was now certain that I was crazy.

My mother and father came for a visit later that day. When they saw our living room, they were appalled, but they didn't rebuke me. Daddy simply asked, "If I buy the materials, will you help me fix it?"

I nodded my head. Daddy returned 30 minutes later with sheetrock, plaster, and paint. We worked the rest of the day repairing the damage. When we finished, the walls looked like new.

My parents never once scolded or chastised me concerning this terrible incident. They obviously knew that their son was not well!

* * *

Joe disliked me intensely, and I was concerned that I might be fired. My concern became reality. After I had worked at the sugar mill for four months, Joe fired me.

During this four-month period I had been drinking at least one six-pack of beer every night. Sometimes I would finish off one six-pack of beer; then I'd have Marsha drive me to a store to buy a second six-pack. Marsha knew that if she didn't drive for me, I would drive myself, so she would usually oblige.

I was very angry about being fired from my job. One night after I had bought a second six-pack, Marsha and I were driving down a main street on our way back to our apartment. We met a car carrying three Hispanic males coming from the opposite direction. The time of day was dusk, and Marsha had just turned on the car lights.

Nearing us, the driver of the other vehicle turned his lights on bright and left them there. After we passed the car, I hung my head out my window and yelled, "You, son-of-a-bitch."

A passenger in the other car yelled something back. The other vehicle turned around, drove up close behind us, and followed us. We turned left at the next intersection, heading for our apartment, and I began to shout, "Pull over, Marsha! Pull over! Pull over!" I felt behind my seat for an empty beer bottle to use as a weapon but didn't find one (the beer I had just purchased was in cans).

I told Marsha that I was going to get a beer bottle, get out of our car, and "settle it with those guys."

Marsha wouldn't pull over. She turned right at the next intersection, then right again into our driveway, and up to our apartment. I jumped out of our car, hurried into the house, grabbed an empty quart beer bottle, and rushed back outside just in time to see the car with the three guys driving down our street very slowly.

I shouted profanities at them and challenged them to a fight. They didn't stop; they just kept going. I was enraged and wanted to fight them all. This instance shows how crazed my mind had become, thanks in part to the alcohol.

On another occasion involving drinking, Marsha and I were sitting in the living room playing the board game Risk with a couple who were friends of ours.

I had drunk several beers. Suddenly I became angry at the other man because he was relentlessly attacking my position on the board. I couldn't understand why he was "singling me out" instead of attacking one of the other players.

All at once, I picked up an ashtray and flung it through a nearby windowpane. Then I grabbed the edge of the game board and upended it, sending dozens of tiny game pieces flying in all directions.

I then walked into the bedroom and flopped down on the bed like a spoiled child. I could hear Marsha in the living room, apologizing to our friends who left shortly thereafter. I called these friends about an hour later and personally apologized for my behavior.

The alcohol was making the OCD tolerable, but the alcohol was becoming more of a problem than the OCD. The alcohol was turning me into a monster. Many months of drinking copious quantities of alcohol drastically altered my personality. Never was this reality more evident in my life than in the following incident:

One night I was drinking beer from my second six-pack and was extremely inebriated. Marsha and I were sitting in the living room conversing when she said something that made me violently angry. I can't remember what she said, but I do know that it was something that wouldn't have angered me had I been sober.

I jumped up from the couch and kicked at our coffee table. My foot struck a leg of the table. The table leg broke off and went flying across the room. I yelled at Marsha: "Now see what you've made me do!"

Marsha was sitting in a cushioned chair. I grabbed her chair and overturned it. Marsha fell to the floor. I quickly grabbed the loose coffee table leg and crouched over her. I swung the wooden leg around and around my head like a madman, threatening to hit her with it, and swearing at her all the while. Marsha was terrified! I didn't strike Marsha, but I was angry enough to have struck her.

I am more ashamed of this incident than anything else I have ever done!

* * *

The reason I've included these horrible, embarrassing episodes in this book is to show how alcohol became a worse enemy than OCD. I had drunk to relieve OCD symptoms. After a time, the alcohol almost became my undoing.

I have since learned this vital lesson: alcohol never solves a problem; it only makes the problem worse or adds another problem. A person struggling with mental illness should *never* drink alcohol to try to solve his or her problems. Mental illness is bad enough without aggravating the condition with alcohol!

Later, with some outside help which I'll discuss in another chapter, I stopped abusing this socially accepted yet deadly drug. If I hadn't, I might not be alive today to tell about it.

19 WORK AND AA

In early 1974 Marsha and I returned to Dallas. We moved into a one-bedroom apartment in the northern part of the city.

I had been drinking heavily for about two years, and I needed help--not only for OCD but for the drinking as well. Marsha had tried to talk me into cutting down on my drinking, but I would tell her time after time, "I would rather be an alcoholic than be neurotic."

Dr. Paschall, my mother's and father's doctor, was to say later, "Reagan, you're using alcohol as medicine." It was true. I treated alcohol as medicine for my tormented mind.

I finally sought help at an AA group in NorthTown Mall in Dallas. The AA members welcomed me with open arms, and I felt comfortable around them.

I had recently landed a good job at a Woolco department store in Dallas as the assistant manager in the automotive department. I was making good money. Marsha was pregnant with our first child, and we were excited about having a baby.

Since joining AA, I had quit drinking and felt good about myself. I had a feeling of accomplishment. However, my OCD was getting worse.

About one month after I joined AA, one of my sponsors found out that I was taking tranquilizers. (Dr. Neely had prescribed Phenobarbital for me. It seemed to calm me down, but it wasn't alleviating my OCD.) The sponsor declared, "You're not sober. You're still high. You've been high all this time on tranquilizers."

His statements brought on stress. I became anxious. I no longer felt proud of myself for quitting drinking. I was now guilt-ridden and distressed. A few days later I was called upon, as is customary, to tell my story at an AA meeting. I no longer was joyful. I felt unworthy!

On the night before I was to talk, I felt nervous. As I sat on the bed in our bedroom, I saw lying on the table beside the bed a publication my mother had sent me, Billy Graham's *Decision*. I picked it up and flipped through the pages. I noticed something about the Devil. Suddenly I became fearful!

For some reason I glanced across the room into the open closet and noticed a bright red shirt of mine hanging there. My mind made a connection! The Devil is usually portrayed as being red. I knew right then that I wouldn't wear that red shirt again.

I started avoiding red at all costs. Not only did I stop wearing that shirt, but I quit wearing anything that was red. If an article of clothing had any hint of red in it, I wouldn't wear it. Many years passed before I would wear a red article of clothing again. Because of this episode I became even more disillusioned and neurotic. I stopped going to AA.

My short exposure to AA, however, ended most of my drinking problems. I believe that AA is one of the most wonderful and helpful organizations in the world. I urge anyone who has a drinking problem not to hesitate to seek help there.

I had made some good friends at AA, and they were wholeheartedly and genuinely interested in helping me with my problem. They did not understand that I had a mental illness, and I did not disclose it to them. The AA establishment is naturally, and for good reason, wary of people taking tranquilizers. Many individuals have become addicted to some types of medication, so there is need for prudence and caution.

AA helped me. I will always have the highest respect for the AA organization, and I am grateful to them for what they did for me.

* * *

I was glad to get the job at Woolco. One of my duties was to label merchandise with price stickers. This procedure had to be repeated frequently; with the high inflation rate of the 1970s, prices were constantly rising.

I hated attaching price stickers because I could rarely attach a sticker to the merchandise in a manner that satisfied my perfectionist tendency. In many instances the sticker would end up either crooked or covering something important. I would feel compelled to straighten or remove it.

The work became tedious and time consuming. I was very frustrated and mentally tired.

I also had to involve myself with much paperwork, and my handwriting obsession-compulsion was giving me trouble. Merchandise was often crooked on the shelves, and I felt the constant need to straighten it. All these compulsions drained me of considerable energy.

Two auto mechanics worked at this Woolco store. I got along fine with one of them, but getting along with the other was difficult. He didn't understand why I should be his boss since he knew more about auto mechanics than I did.

The constant price changing of the merchandise, the paperwork, and the troublesome mechanic were making me increasingly anxious, and my OCD was becoming crippling. After four weeks of anguish, I could no longer tolerate the constant high level of stress, and I resigned. Marsha was very supportive of me, but I felt like a failure.

We needed money, and I immediately began job hunting. I was quickly hired to a job earning minimum wage at Skillern's Drugs in Dallas. The Woolco assistant manager's job had paid well, and regressing to minimum wage was disheartening!

The month was August. School was about to begin, and school supplies were flooding into the drugstore.

One of my first job assignments was to build a cubic figure about six feet by six feet by four feet out of bundles of notebook paper. They had to be stacked neatly, but the OCD made me take more pains than normal to perform this job.

The task became grueling work. I had literally hundreds of paper bundles to stack, and I was compelled to adjust the position of almost every bundle several times before my crazed mind would be satisfied. Stacking the bundles of paper required a much longer time than would have been required by an ordinary individual. I'm sure this fact didn't sit well with my boss, but he didn't say anything. When the job was finally accomplished, I was emotionally exhausted.

Sometimes I was sent to work in the photo department. I despised this duty also because, at the time, the Kodak film company was running ads reading: "A picture is forever." *Forever* was one of my *bad words*, so I was under additional stress while working in that department. I just wanted to get away from that word *forever*.

Life was a constant struggle.

* * *

During this difficult period Marsha and I had moved into an apartment complex in north Dallas. We needed a couch for our unfurnished apartment.

Marsha located an ad in the newspaper describing a couch that an individual had for sale at a low price. We decided to drive to that person's house to look at the couch.

The couch was a nice one for the money, and we informed the woman that we would buy it. She said she could not accept money on that particular day, Saturday, due to her religion. She said we could take the couch, but we would have to come back the following day to pay. I immediately recoiled at this revelation. I fought what I knew were irrational feelings.

We took the couch to our apartment and set it in the living room.

I can't explain exactly what happened inside me. I think the strange feelings I experienced had to do with my concluding that the woman had a strange religion; her not being able to accept money on Saturday troubled me. My perceived peculiarity of her belief caused the couch to become *tainted.* I could no longer enjoy sitting on it or looking at it. All I could think about was getting rid of that couch.

After much torment, I told Marsha that I had decided that I didn't like the couch, and I would like to return it. I lied. I really did like the looks of the couch, and it was a bargain for the money. I was filled with anguish and sorrow because I had to say that I wanted to return the couch although my reasons were completely irrational and I myself did not understand them.

After some mild debate, Marsha reluctantly agreed to return the couch to the woman. We took it back the next day.

* * *

I quit my job at Skillern's after about a month for the same reasons that had caused me to resign from the Woolco job. I just couldn't handle a job. I was too sick!

20 THE CONFRONTATION

Marsha went into labor early one morning. The date was September 17, 1974. I drove her to Parkland Hospital, and our son Paul was born.

After her stay in the hospital, we moved from our north Dallas apartment into Marsha's mother's home in Irving. We could no longer pay the rent on our apartment.

Not having to worry about paying rent was comforting for a while, but before long the positives of the new housing arrangement began to be outweighed by the negatives.

As soon as she was able, Marsha began working as a checker at Krogers.

I stayed home with the baby all day. I virtually lived in our bedroom.

Sharon and Lisa, Marsha's older sisters, also lived there in that four-bedroom house, along with Don, her brother. Friends of the family frequently came over to the house to visit, but I rarely came out of the bedroom when there were guests. I didn't want to face or socialize with any visitors, so embarrassed and humiliated was I for having failed at three jobs and for not being able to work and support my family.

We lived in that house for almost a year while Marsha and Sharon worked to support the whole family. Lisa was unable to work due to a handicap; Don worked sporadically in the siding business.

Marsha's mother did much of the housework and prepared the meals. She also received help from Marsha, Sharon, and Lisa with these chores. I felt like the most useless member of the family, and accumulating guilt rose steadily in me as time passed.

Whenever other members of the family would become upset or angry about something, they would usually voice their feelings. I, however, never expressed any anger or feelings of any kind. I felt that I was "mooching" off Marsha's family and that I didn't deserve to let myself be heard voicing an opinion about any issue that might arise.

An undesirable situation can be created when one dams up all his/her feelings and emotions inside and never ventilates.

Marsha and I had been living at her mother's house for about a year when late one night Don, who drank heavily at the time and was drunk, began to badger Brookie, his mother. Don, Marsha, Brookie, and I were all sitting in the living room. I, too, had been drinking, or else the confrontation would probably not have occurred.

Don began saying, in his drunken state: "Sing me a song, Mother, sing me a song."

He repeated this statement over and over again for several minutes, and finally I could stand no more. I believe that my pent-up emotions just finally had to burst to the forefront.

I jumped wildly from my chair and started across the room toward Don. Brookie, who was seated between us and over to the side a bit, arose and took a step forward to intervene. By accident, I partially collided with Brookie, forcing her backward into her chair.

As I approached Don, I screamed, "Try making me sing a song!" I rushed up to him and forcefully pushed him backward into his chair.

Brookie began to shout, "Stop it! Stop it!"

Don immediately rose to his feet and declared that he had no argument with me. He said, "Reagan, you're like a brother to me."

I hesitated. Don was making peace! He then grabbed my hand in a friendly handshake.

In the meantime, Brookie was emotionally distressed by my violent outburst, and she began having chest pain. Marsha, who was still years away from entering nursing school, began trying to comfort her mother. We all began to focus our attention upon Brookie.

A registered nurse lived down the street, and Marsha and I ran to get her. The nurse came back with us and examined Brookie. She concluded that Brookie's heart wasn't causing the pain. Brookie had no history of heart trouble. Soon the nurse returned home.

I voiced the opinion that Brookie should go to the hospital as a precautionary measure. Don was opposed. Soon a heated argument ensued between Don and me concerning whether or not Brookie should go to the hospital. Don began shouting and cursing at me, declaring emphatically, in his inebriated condition, that his mother didn't need an ambulance or a hospital!

I became very stubborn, and even though Don protested, I picked up the phone in the dining room and called an ambulance. Brookie was taken to the hospital, where doctors determined that she was having a heart attack.

I wasn't proud of myself!

After spending a few days in the hospital, Brookie returned home in reasonably good health.

I would like to add that, in spite of this particular difficulty, Don in most instances was like a big brother to me.

Soon afterward, Marsha and I traveled back to the Rio Grande Valley and moved in with my mother and father.

21 PERFECTION TO THE LETTER

One of my main problems became what I call a "pathological perfectionist tendency." I did not want to attempt something unless I thought I could do it perfectly. I realized before long that I couldn't do anything perfectly, so I just would not attempt to create anything. Beginning in my early teens, my creativity slid steadily downhill to near bottom.

Later, when I became a teacher at the age of thirty, I was not a creative person at all. I had not used any of the creative juices within myself for many years.

To be a successful teacher, one must be resourceful, and I was afraid to try anything imaginative or inventive. I had not "created" anything since the Styrofoam deer at age thirteen. That horrific episode with the deer had made me intensely reluctant to pursue anything creative.

This creative void was an enormous stumbling block for me in becoming an effective teacher. I had to rekindle within myself that imaginative spirit that had lain dormant for so many years.

Developing originality in my life again was very difficult although I had in my early years considered myself artistically talented, before my illness became so consuming.

I could copy someone else's idea if I thought it had merit, and OCD wouldn't bother me. But my own creativity was a big problem.

* * *

Here are examples of some OCD symptoms I had.

Every night I wanted my shoes to be lined up just right. When I laid my shoes on the floor at night before going to bed, I had to set them with the right shoe a little bit ahead of the left shoe. I blame this symptom on my once having read that the word *right* meant skillful, and the word *left* meant sinister.

I began trying to perform tasks so that the *right side* seemed to dominate. Doing this made me less anxious. I would use my right hand and avoid using my left as much as possible.

I even practiced chewing my food with the right side of my mouth. Not to do these things was to feel uncomfortable.

* * *

If I tore a paper out of a spiral notebook and a little paper tag hung from the page, I felt compelled to remove the tag. Everything had to be perfectly neat.

* * *

As a teenager on our farm, I was asked at times to drive a tractor or a cotton picker. I remember experiences such as plowing a field of cotton stalks, then seeing a stalk left sticking up in the area I had already plowed. This would drive me crazy. I would want to jump down off the tractor and go fix it!

Scenarios such as the *unplowed cotton stalks* and the *pig pen rituals* occurred many times in my youth and convinced me absolutely that I did not want to follow in my father's footsteps and become a farmer.

I also had trouble with shop class in high school. If I didn't weld something *perfectly,* my OCD would flare-up and would make me miserable.

I just couldn't do anything creative because my creation would always seem *flawed* and cause additional apprehension and unhappiness.

I loved to draw pictures when in grade school. As an adult I have always envied artists. In my early youth I had believed that I had potential in that area. I've known for a long time, however, that I couldn't paint pictures. I've never attempted to paint because of my belief that, if I tried to paint a picture, I would become obsessed by some detail that disturbed me. I wouldn't be able to enjoy my creation. I'd think I had put a little too much paint here or not enough there. I might not have a certain color just right.

For a person like me who has difficulty with simple things like *handwriting* and wants to go back and correct letters, painting would be out of the question!

Reading was also not immune to this craziness. I became a very slow reader because, while reading, I needed to pronounce each word mentally. I would frequently go back and reread a section in order to have read it *right*--to have absorbed all the meaning and not missed any detail.

I still have some of these symptoms today, but I've learned to live with them – and around them.

22 TEACHING IN LAREDO

After Marsha and I moved in with my mother and father, I immediately began to improve emotionally, due partly, I think, to my idea that I was now on my home turf and had a right to express my true feelings.

This was in September 1975. The following January, with Marsha's and my mother's urgings, I at age 29 enrolled at Texas A & I University in Kingsville where I began preparation to become a teacher. The college was about 80 miles from home, and I commuted three days a week until May. I earned an emergency teaching certificate after completing twelve hours in education courses.

I applied to several school districts in South Texas and landed a teaching job to begin in September 1976 at a junior high school in Laredo.

The summer before I started teaching, I worked for Charlie and Robert Hoot, the farmers who leased my father's acreage. I found something mentally soothing and comforting about working out in the fields 12 to 15 hours a day, and my health improved.

I had earned enough money to get Marsha and me off to a good start in Laredo. We moved in August, and I began teaching life science to seventh graders in a junior high school with over 1,800 students. We lived in a tiny garage apartment that we rented for $85 per month.

The handwriting obsession bothered me so much that I asked Marsha to grade all my students' papers during my first year of teaching. I didn't dare look too closely at the students' papers that first year. I was concerned that I would develop a handwriting obsession about *their handwriting* which might lead to a powerful urge to correct imperfect letters on *their papers*. I surmised that, if this ever happened, it would probably doom my aspirations to become a successful teacher! I will be forever grateful to Marsha for finding time to grade all my papers that first year. She was working as a checker at Krogers, but somehow she found the time to help me.

* * *

In the early 1970s the movie *The Exorcist* had been playing in theaters across the nation. I didn't know what an exorcist was or what the movie was about, but I asked Marsha if she would like to see it. She declined. I found out later that the movie concerned a girl becoming possessed by the Devil. I found this to be a disturbing idea, and I never went to see the movie. However, *The Exorcist* was eventually to have a profound impact on my life.

The obsession concerning the Devil began slowly. After a time, however, this obsession began bothering me so much that I began trying to avoid the words *Devil* and *Satan* and anything remotely connected with them.

Later, whenever I would think the words *The Exorcist*, I would mentally say "*The French Connection*" and "*Fiddler on the Roof*" twice to cancel out the *bad words*. *The French Connection* and *Fiddler on the Roof* seemed to me good, non-anxiety-provoking movies that I had seen and liked, and their titles, to my warped way of thinking, had the power to cancel out the *bad words*. I performed this mental ritual hundreds of times over the years!

* * *

My teaching job went fairly smoothly for about three years.

Marsha and I attended church on just two occasions in the five years we lived in Laredo. I wanted to go to church, but I feared what I might hear there.

On one occasion I summoned my courage, and we attended the Sunday worship service of a fairly large Episcopal church. I was enjoying the service when, toward the end of the sermon, the priest mentioned the word *Satan*. I recoiled at the mere mention of that word! So severe and unpleasant was my reaction that I didn't attend another church service for about four years.

More trouble began when I was watching a science program on television one summer day and the narrator said something about "when the universe began..."

I remember being shocked and thinking, "I thought the universe had always been here. I didn't know it had a beginning."

This narrator's statement had an intense effect upon me. I guess I had forgotten the first page of Genesis in the Bible: "In the beginning, God created the heavens and the earth..." I had been familiar with this scripture all my life, and that passage clearly indicates that the universe had a beginning. But remembering that passage didn't help. I couldn't get the idea out of my head that the universe had had a *beginning*. I thought about it every day. I tried hard, but I couldn't dislodge this persistent thought! For some peculiar reason, which contradicts what the Bible teaches in Genesis, I found that this new idea (at least it seemed new to me) that the universe had had a beginning was causing me to lose faith in God and the Bible. I even begin to question whether God really existed. I didn't want to question it! I had always believed in God. But I simply couldn't help myself.

Losing faith in God was scary to me! Before, I had believed that the Lord had always helped me in difficult times. Now, it seemed, the source of all my strength and hope was evaporating. I desperately prayed for help, but nothing happened, except that I fell deeper and deeper into this obsession which seemed a bottomless pit.

At the same time the situation in my classroom at school began falling apart. I tried to teach, but all I could think about was my obsession about whether or not God existed. I walked around the classroom as if in a daze, partially unaware of much that was taking place around me.

Kids catch on quickly if something is amiss. I began to lose control of my classroom. Students began misbehaving.

I was so preoccupied and troubled that on a couple of occasions my tests contained only 5 questions; even then, writing and grading those short tests was rigorous for me.

The students weren't learning much because I wasn't teaching much. I was too sick! I don't blame the students. Students will misbehave if they find that attending a certain class is a waste of time.

I had chewing gum thrown at me while I was writing on the chalkboard. It would become caught in my hair, and Marsha would have to cut it out at home.

The legs of the students' desks were held on by screws, and students were constantly removing the screws so that the legs would fall off, then hiding the screws and saying that the legs just fell off all by themselves. I knew better, but I had a difficult time stopping this practice.

Once the trash in the wastebasket in my classroom was set on fire. A fellow teacher had to put it out with a fire extinguisher.

Newly refurbished tables that were placed in my room were desecrated in the short period of a few weeks as students scratched notes and initials into their surfaces. The assistant principal came to my room and observed the damage that had been done to the surfaces of the tables and stated that he couldn't believe that I could allow that to happen in my classroom. The truth is I don't remember even one student's scratching the tops of those tables, so overwhelming was my preoccupation with obsessive thoughts.

Once a student put masking tape on the lens of a projector I was attempting to use to show a filmstrip, and about 20 minutes of the class period was wasted before I discovered what the problem was.

The mental ailment, the obsession I couldn't get rid of, was destroying my ability to manage my classroom effectively. I had taught in the same classroom for three years previously without any major discipline problems. But now my illness was allowing the tearing apart of my classroom and my career!

Some of the rowdier boys began yelling *joto* at me from afar when I would be walking to my classroom in the morning or away from it after school. (*Joto*, pronounced *hoto*, is a Spanish word that means *homosexual*. This word is about the vilest name that an Hispanic child can call an adult male. About 95% of my students were Hispanic.)

The head principal never once entered my classroom during this time. Even if he had, it's doubtful that he could have helped me since the root of the problem in my classroom was my mental illness.

I knew I needed to see a doctor, but Laredo had no psychiatrists. The closest psychiatrists were in San Antonio, which was 158 miles away. I called Dr. Neely in Dallas, and he recommended two psychiatrists in San Antonio.

I chose Dr. Johnson* and scheduled an appointment with him. I liked him initially. He enjoyed analyzing dreams, and at each session he would ask me about my dreams.

Once I told him about an extremely bizarre dream I had in which I was hanging upside down in the nude in his office and, while talking to him, had an orgasm and ejaculated. The sexual nature of the dream was embarrassing to relate to him, but I went ahead, thinking there

---

* name changed

might be something there that was important for him to know.

He immediately began to probe to determine if I might be gay, but he proceeded in a very subtle manner. He had found out that I loved football, and he began describing three gay football players whom he claimed he had treated. He said they played for a prominent professional football team and assured me that there was nothing wrong with being gay.

I was totally turned off by this line of questioning. I quickly informed the good doctor that there was no possibility that I was gay.

Although I don't despise homosexuals and, on the contrary, believe that they have been treated unfairly by much of society, I was offended by Dr. Johnson's inferences that I might be gay.

The most significant thing that this doctor did was to hurt further my faith in God. Mentally ill people can be very vulnerable to suggestion, especially if the suggestion comes from someone whom the patient holds in high esteem, someone like a psychiatrist.

I told this doctor that I was having obsessions about the Devil which were troubling me considerably. He informed me that his mother had been a devout Christian and his father an atheist. He stated, "If you don't believe in a god, then you don't have to believe in a devil." This philosophy seemed to be his simple prescription for my getting rid of this obsession.

I never booked another appointment with Dr. Johnson. Instead of helping me, his *therapy* was probably one of the reasons that I became *destined* for the mental ward at Valley Baptist Medical Center in Harlingen.

At this point I was really confused about whether or not God existed. I had always, since early childhood, had the habit of praying before going to sleep at night. Now my mind was so troubled that concentrating on prayer became difficult. I became so anxious and perplexed about religion that I told Marsha that I was just going to consider myself an agnostic and not worry about God anymore. She shot back, "No, Reagan! You have always believed and trusted in God, and you shouldn't change." Marsha's response helped me. But the worst was yet to come.

The notion began slowly creeping into my mind that I might be "possessed by the Devil." After the movie *The Exorcist*, many devil movies were being made. Watching the constant advertising on TV was agonizing.

When one of these movie ads would come on TV, I would rush up to the set and change the channel.

When Marsha and I would go to the movies, I would wait in the lobby until all the movie previews had been shown; then Marsha would come out of the theater and get me.

This "devil movie" craze was exactly that to me. It was driving me crazy! I remembered the story in the Bible of the time when Jesus cured the madman. The story described how the demons that had possessed him had come out and entered into a herd of pigs, and how the pigs had gone mad and rushed into a body of water. I hoped that I wasn't possessed!

One of the main things that helped me remain halfway sane during this trying time was the writing of Norman Vincent Peale. I believe I read every one of his books. Dr. Peale's blend of religion and psychiatry in his books brought me great comfort.

At his church in New York City, Dr. Peale worked with a team of psychiatrists who were Christians. I will never forget the wonderful and powerful messages in his books.

In one book, he described *demons* such as fear, worry, guilt, and anger which could possess people. This made sense to me and consoled me by helping me feel that maybe I wasn't possessed by *supernatural demons* after all, but was simply afflicted by demons such as *worry* and *fear*. After reading this section in his book, I became wonderfully joyous and relieved. However, my phobia concerning the Devil persisted for many more years and took several new forms.

* * *

Marsha and I ordered a new Chrysler LeBaron in 1977. We chose a white exterior and a blue interior. I couldn't wait for the car to arrive.

Several weeks before the car arrived, I for some reason started associating the color *blue* with *hell*. I think these thoughts began after I had read somewhere that hell had blue flames in it, and I thought about the blue flames of a gas stove or oven.

Shortly afterward, I became unhappy about the fact that our new car was to have a blue interior. Every time I would think about the joy of getting a new car, my mind would associate the blue interior with *hell* and the *Devil*. I couldn't even enjoy getting a new automobile. My diseased mind wouldn't allow it!

I had always been an avid sports fan. About this time the Duke University Blue Devils basketball team was playing well and was getting frequent publicity in the newspapers and on TV. Hearing time after time about the *Blue Devils* made me even more anxious about the car we had ordered. Whenever I heard the words *Blue Devils*, I would mentally say the words *blue sky, blue sky* to cancel out the *bad words*. I was substituting a thought that wasn't anxiety provoking for one that was. I performed that mental ritual scores of times over a period of several months.

When the new automobile did arrive, I was excited, but mine was a tempered excitement. When riding in the car, I would have to perform many mental rituals to feel comfortable. Much of the joy that getting a new car should have provided was lost.

Dr. Neely had recommended another psychiatrist in San Antonio at the same time he had recommended Dr. Johnson, and I began seeing Dr. McCallum.* I told him about my conflicts concerning religion and the Devil, and he carefully wrote everything down on paper. He prescribed some medication for me that never worked, but the main thing he advised me to do was jog. Dr. McCallum claimed he had treated a priest who had OCD similar to mine and that jogging had cured him.

I began to jog. I jogged and jogged. This was useless. My mental state became progressively worse. I considered it puzzling that the doctor had spent four years in college, four years in medical school, one year as an intern, and two to three years specializing in psychiatry, and that all he was telling me to do was jog!

* * *

Marsha and I have always enjoyed Christmas. One evening close to Christmas Day, Marsha came home from work carrying two new Christmas albums which she had just purchased. We both loved Christmas carols. I put one on the stereo to play.

We were both happily enjoying the music when, about halfway through the first album, the word *Satan* was mentioned in one of the Christmas carols. I froze. What had started out as a good time suddenly turned ugly. I realized that I could not allow this album with that *awful word* in my house, and I asked Marsha please to take the album out and throw it away. We began to argue. I walked out the front door in a fit of anger, got into my car, and drove away. Our wonderful evening was completely spoiled by my twisted thoughts. While I was gone, Marsha

---

* name changed

reluctantly threw the new Christmas album into the trash can.

The obsessions about God, the Devil, and religion became more severe. I reached the point that I couldn't sleep at night, and I would lie awake with thoughts circulating through my head about there not being a God. I would think about stories from the Bible, and my uncontrolled mind would think up all sorts of reasons that the Bible stories couldn't be true. This train of thought made me more anxiety-ridden than I had ever been before. I also began to fear the Devil more than ever. My losing faith in God and the Bible made this my worst obsession ever!

I went to see Dr. McCallum in San Antonio and was so mentally agitated that I couldn't sit down. I rapidly paced back and forth in his office like a caged animal. Dr. McCallum didn't seem concerned, and he recommended that I increase my jogging.

I did, but to no avail. I called him later from Laredo and informed him that I was getting desperate, and he increased my medication. This medicine had never worked, and the increased dosage didn't accomplish any positive results either.

I became increasingly anxious. I was getting only two to three hours of sleep per night, and the rest of the nighttime was spent with my lying in bed, wide awake with obsessive thoughts swirling through my head. Days, then weeks, then months passed with my being almost totally unable to sleep. Insomnia is an awful affliction, especially when hour after hour is spent lying in bed with the unhappiest thoughts imaginable flowing through one's mind without any means of stopping the flow!

Over-the-counter sleeping pills didn't help. Then I tried alcohol. I would pull my exhausted but wide-awake body out of bed at two or three o'clock in the morning, go to the kitchen, and drink two or three cans of beer while watching TV. Then I would go back to bed and again try to go to sleep. But sleep wouldn't come. After several months, my mind and body felt as if they were coming unraveled.

The situation at school was equally abhorrent. The kids in my classroom were having their way, and disciplining them became impossible. I couldn't control my life, much less concentrate on making my students mind.

One afternoon, in total desperation, I phoned my mother and stammered: "Mama, is it normal to spend several hours of each day thinking about and being afraid of the Devil?"

She exclaimed, "No, it isn't."

I tried to explain what was happening with me. She said, "I think maybe you should go to Harlingen and check yourself into the hospital."

I thanked her for her advice and hung up the phone. I called Dr. McCallum in San Antonio and asked him if he would admit me to a hospital in San Antonio. He told me that he was sorry, but he didn't run a hospital practice. I asked him if he thought I could receive help in a hospital, and he replied that he thought it was possible.

When Marsha came home from work that day, I told her that I wanted to check myself into Valley Baptist Medical Center in Harlingen, about three and a half hours away. She agreed that that sounded like a good idea.

I called my mother back and asked her if she would arrange for me to be admitted the next day to the hospital. She said she would be glad to.

I immediately felt relieved! My mother called Dr. Paschall, and he took care of the details.

The next morning, Marsha drove me to the hospital in Harlingen, and I was admitted to the psychiatric wing. That night, a nurse gave me a powerful sleeping pill. I got a full, blissful night's sleep for the first time in months, and I was able to rest my very weary mind!

Even though he wasn't a psychiatrist, Dr. Paschall was my doctor. While in the hospital, I slept well every night, thanks to the sleeping pills. Dr. Paschall placed me on the medications Thorazine and Tofranil, which helped relieve my anxiety and diminish my obsessions, and I began thinking more clearly.

I also smoked like a chimney. Once while making rounds, Dr. Paschall found my room so full of cigarette smoke that he turned to his partner Dr. Harris and remarked: "Break out the cue sticks!"

To this day, when I look back on my three-week stay at the Harlingen hospital, I view it mainly as a restful, healing experience. The World Series was played in its entirety while I was there, and this event gave me something to watch on TV. And I was visited by my uncle Raymond who boosted my ego.

Marsha stayed in Laredo because of work and nursing school, but she drove to see me when she could.

One day my mother came to visit and brought me a potted plant. I was shocked! I asked her, "What's the name of that plant?" I already knew.

She responded, "Devil's Ivy."

I said, "Please get rid of it!"

She looked at me quizzically at first, then appeared to understand; she removed the plant.

Some of the nurses became my friends. There was one middle-aged female nurse of whom I became particularly fond. I didn't care for her at first because I considered her to be too brisk and matter-of-fact. But she was to help me significantly.

I'll never forget what she said when I confided in her that I was having trouble with religion and in believing in God. Pointing out the window at the beautiful landscaped scene, she remarked, "Look at those palm trees. Even they are a miracle. How can you look out this window at them and not believe in God?"

That's the way she was. I believe she was sent directly from the *Creator* to help heal my disoriented mind!

During the day I would attend therapy class with a group of troubled individuals. The different patients would talk about their problems and discuss them with each other. I would listen, but I did not take part in the conversation. Right or wrong, I considered my problem concerning religion too personal to discuss with these strangers. But I was comforted in being with other individuals who were suffering from mental problems.

At a certain time of the day, we would all go to a therapy workshop to make Christmas ornaments. I didn't really enjoy this activity, and it was still a fairly long time before Christmas, but I dutifully attended the class and made ornaments.

This therapy, although boring, may have helped me more than I realized. After about two weeks, a nurse took me for a walk outside the hospital once or twice.

After three weeks in the hospital, I was well enough to go home to Laredo and complete the school year.

I continued on the medications Dr. Paschall prescribed for me. Although they didn't cure me, they were a step in the right direction. The heavy dosages, however, made me so drowsy that I would sometimes fall asleep when I was alone in the teachers' lounge during my conference period.

Discipline in my classroom remained bad the following year. I could not seem to get the kids to behave. I guess they had misbehaved for too long in my classroom, and this lack of discipline set an bad precedent and caused me to get an unfavorable reputation as a teacher.

Looking back on this period, I am surprised that I was able to continue. One of the main reasons I had the strength to endure was that I called in sick every Wednesday, like clockwork. That gave me a break in the middle of the week and kept me going. I'm truly amazed that I didn't get fired for missing so much school, but at the time teachers were hard to come by in Laredo. That fact probably saved my job, but my paycheck each month was seriously short.

Julie, my next to the youngest child, was born during this grueling period. She was delivered during the week, and I used this occasion as an excuse to miss three days of school.

Julie's birth was a double blessing: a beautiful daughter and a way to get away from that horrible classroom situation for a brief period.

23 THE BAD WORDS

Over the years certain words, and the ideas they represented, became anxiety provoking for me. Although there are also many others, some examples are the words *time*, *mind*, *eternity*, *forever*, *death*, *exorcist*, and *devil*.

When I began dating my first wife, Debbie, she was in high school and I was in college. Debbie informed me one day that her English teacher wanted each student in the class to write a definition for the word *time* without using a dictionary. Almost everyone is aware of how often this word is used in everyday conversation in such phrases as "What *time* is it?" or "It's *time* to go." *Time* is one of the most commonly used words in the English language.

Debbie asked me if I could help her. At first I thought that this task would be easy. After all, *time* is a common word.

I began trying to think of a suitable definition. I thought and thought. Before long I realized that defining *time* was not simple after all. I racked my brain, and I still couldn't come up with an appropriate definition.

When Debbie had initially asked me to help her with this definition, I thought, "Here's an ideal opportunity for me, a college student, to impress my high school girlfriend with my superior abilities." But, to my dismay, I began to feel embarrassed by my inability to define the word.

Time didn't become a bad word for me then, but this was the beginning.

One day several years later I began thinking about how I hadn't been readily able to define this word. I decided to look it up in the dictionary. The dictionary contained a definition similar to this one: "The measured or measurable period during which action, process, or condition exists or continues: duration."

This definition seemed rather vague to me. I still couldn't get a handle on the real meaning of the concept *time*. I asked myself what exactly was meant by the words *period* and *duration*? I began to regard the word *time* as a somewhat mysterious and abstract concept.

Listening to my car radio one day, I heard the word *time* as the last word spoken before I turned off the radio. I felt uncomfortable. I suddenly didn't want that to be the last word I heard spoken on the radio. I turned the radio on again. I listened for a moment, then switched it off again. The last word spoken was some word other than *time*. For some strange reason I now felt relieved.

Not much later a new television program named *Sixty Minutes* began to be aired on TV. The program commenced with the sound of a ticking clock. The *ticking* of a clock had never bothered me before, but now it was creating uneasiness in me.

Marsha and I were at her sister Cindy's house one evening when *Sixty Minutes* began. I suddenly couldn't bear the sound of that ticking clock. The *ticking* reminded me of the abstract concept *time*. Also, the title of this program, *Sixty Minutes*, was about *time*. I hurried out of the living room where the TV was and into the kitchen--just to get away from that ticking clock.

For many years I wouldn't watch *Sixty Minutes* just because of its title and the sound of the ticking clock. Only in recent years have I been able to watch this TV show without its creating mental anguish and stress in me.

In a similar fashion, the word *mind* became one of my *bad words*. A college professor of mine once asked if anyone could tell exactly what was meant by the word *mind*. The first thought that came into my mind (pardon the pun) was the word *brain*. But then I realized that *mind* and *brain* are not the same.

Mind was another difficult concept to define and internalize. Its meaning became mysterious to me, and the *mysteriousness* somehow spawned *fearfulness*. For an unknown reason, *mind*'s obscure meaning made the word frightening. I guess this type of fear could be called "fear of the unknown." This was similar to the fear some individuals have of heights or of flying in airplanes.

From that day forth, whenever I would use the word *mind* in a sentence, I wouldn't want that to be the last *word* I spoke. If it was, I'd say another word to *cancel* the *bad word*. On many occasions I'd whisper the other word very softly "under my breath" so that the person I was speaking to wouldn't hear or notice anything peculiar (at least I hoped no one would notice).

I remember when I was very young, I would sometimes think about the idea of living *forever*. Having been raised a Christian, I wondered what it would be like to live in heaven *forever*. I would let my imagination toy with this concept. I'd try to picture how long *forever* was. This mental activity was fun at first. I would think and think, trying my best to visualize *forever* in my mind.

After toying with this idea for several minutes, I would suddenly feel mildly panicked, acknowledging that *forever* is never-ending, a concept that I couldn't fathom. *Forever* hadn't yet become a *bad word*. Not until I became an adult did this word begin to trouble my neurotic mind.

After *forever* became a *bad word*, I dropped it from my speech. I would not utter this word! Nor would I write it. Related words also became *bad words*, words such as *eternity*, *infinity* and *never*.

My reaction to the movie *The Exorcist* made the words *devil* and *exorcist* into *bad words*. Before long the word *demon* entered this category.

I tried to shut bad words and their concepts completely out of my mind and out of my life. When I found this to be impossible, I invented magical rituals to cancel-out these words. The rituals worked well in removing the pain and apprehension that the *bad words* caused. But I had to perform these rituals frequently--whenever and wherever I encountered these *words*--whether they were in a newspaper or in a song or spoken by another person.

I encountered the most difficulty, however, when I would *think* a *bad word.* I would have to perform a mental ritual to cancel out the *bad thought.* Since thoughts are impossible for a person who has OCD to control, the *bad thoughts* were especially troublesome!

Whenever I would think a *bad word* like *forever*, I would initiate a ritual to cancel it out. I would whisper something to myself like "yes, yes--yes, yes" to cancel out the *bad word.*

Yes was a non-anxiety-provoking, good, positive word. Four *yes*'s equaled two pair—"two and two" for perfect symmetry. Perfect symmetry was a comfort zone for me.

I don't know why the word *yes* had the power to cancel out the anxiety brought about by the bad word *forever*, but OCD doesn't usually make much sense.

I practiced what might be called *censored thinking.* I couldn't stop the *bad words* from invading my thoughts, so I *censored* them by using rituals to cancel them out.

24 OCD: ROUGH ON A MARRIAGE

OCD often ruined what should have been good times for Marsha and me. One example began early one Saturday morning. Marsha, our young son Paul, and I set out in our car for Garner State Park, located in the Texas Hill Country about 170 miles north of Laredo. The Frio River runs through the park, and enormous trees grow along its banks. There are paddle boats, a miniature golf course, camping facilities, steep climbing hills, and other attractions. The park is a beautiful place. Marsha had never been to the park, and I was enthusiastic about showing it to her.

About ten miles into our journey, we stopped at a convenience store to get gas. As we drove away from the store, Marsha reached into a bag and pulled out a roll of LifeSavers candy. She offered one to me. I looked at what she was offering. I cringed! What disturbed me about the LifeSavers doesn't make much sense.

The word *LifeSavers* was one of my *bad words*. Why *LifeSavers* was a *bad word* is difficult to explain. I'm not sure that even I understand. But here's my guess:

At the opposite end of "saving a life" is "losing a life." "Losing a life" refers to *death*, which was a *bad word* of mine. Maybe that's the connection my mind made. The word *LifeSavers* reminded me of the word *death*. So in my mind, the word *LifeSavers* became a *bad word* also.

When I was a child, my parents would frequently buy LifeSavers for my sister and me. I loved them. As an adult, after *LifeSavers* became a *bad word*, I avoided this candy.

Marsha was unaware that this word or the candy bothered me. She didn't know that many years had passed since I had eaten a piece of LifeSavers candy.

My being this *crazy* was embarrassing and humiliating! I didn't want to admit my true feelings. I couldn't feel comfortable with that *wretched* roll of candy in the car. My solution was to get angry.

How could Marsha do such a thing as bring that *awful* candy into my presence? (Marsha had always been considerate of my *crazy* emotions, but only when she was aware of those emotions.)

I didn't stop to think that she was totally unaware of my irrational feeling toward *LifeSavers* candy. To me she seemed inconsiderate in *aggravating* my OCD as she was doing. I reacted as if I thought she had deliberately purchased the *LifeSavers* to spoil my trip!

Now, when I look back upon this incident, I realize that Marsha would *never* have deliberately tried to agitate my mental illness.

I remember that I was dealing with a sick mind and that sick minds don't think sensibly.

I began to lash out at Marsha: "Why are you buying that hard candy?" I scolded. "Don't you know that it will rot your teeth! Hard candy is the worst kind of candy to eat because it coats your teeth with sugar. Bacteria grow in that sugar and produce acids that eat away at your tooth enamel!"

I went on and on with my chastising. I was substituting what sounded like a rational reason to get rid of the candy for the real reason which was irrational.

Subconsciously, I probably thought that, if I tried to explain the real reason I objected to LifeSavers candy, I wouldn't make sense, and I wouldn't be able to make Marsha understand.

Of course, Marsha became very angry with the manner in which I was speaking to her. (And she had a good reason to be angry!)

At the time, however, I guess I thought it better that she become angry with me than to know the truth, as long as she got rid of that candy.

As a result of OCD, Marsha and I didn't speak to each other the rest of the two and a half hour trip to Garner State Park. We didn't speak until we had been in the park for over half an hour.

OCD ruined what would have been many other good times in our marriage. If Marsha weren't such a patient and understanding individual, she wouldn't have stayed married to me beyond a few years.

In fact, she probably never would have married me at all.

25 STRUGGLING TO VICTORY

A fresh start teaching began in Harlingen, a town of approximately 50 thousand people located in deep South Texas about 350 miles south of Houston.

The last year and a half in Laredo had been horrible. In Harlingen I was hired to teach eighth grade at Memorial Junior High.

I had never done student teaching. I hadn't learned much about teaching in Laredo due to my OCD problems there, and I had feared being creative. I hoped in Harlingen to learn how to become an effective teacher.

Mr. Sheffield, the personnel director for the Harlingen Independent School District, interviewed me. He asked if my teaching contract in Laredo had been renewed. I told him that Laredo hadn't sent me a contract yet, but that I expected that they would.

He asked, "You weren't fired, were you?"

I assured him, "No, I wasn't fired."

Mr. Sheffield hired me to teach eighth grade life and earth science. After we moved to Harlingen, I never received any word from Laredo.

My first two years in Harlingen went reasonably well. Toward the middle of my third year, I began to become very anxious.

At this time I was attending the University of Texas at Brownsville and working on my master's degree in education. The teaching plus the college involvement was keeping me very busy.

The junior high where I taught had a system of classroom management called "assertive discipline." One of the minor facets of this program was that, when a student would get caught misbehaving, the teacher would write his/her name on the chalkboard without making any comment. If that student broke a class rule again that same period, a checkmark would be placed beside his/her name. For each infraction, he/she would get an additional checkmark. One check would mean a 15-minute detention after school, two checks a 30-minute detention, etc.

This system worked well for me for over two years. The third year the system began to break down and become ineffective for me. I discussed this issue with a teacher colleague. She advised me to discontinue the system.

But I didn't discontinue it. This was a system of discipline that had worked for me for two years, and I tenaciously clung to it. I reasoned that, if I didn't use the system, the situation in Harlingen might deteriorate as it had in Laredo. That thought was abhorrent.

The situation got very bad during the second semester of that third year. I would write students' names on the board and add checks for additional misbehavior, but this wouldn't do any good. The students just kept misbehaving. I became extremely exasperated.

Then I learned that the following year life science would be dropped as an eighth grade course, and I would be teaching earth science all year. I began to feel very insecure about how I was going to *stretch* what had previously been a one-semester course into two semesters.

As the semester progressed, the anxiety continued to build.

Then something new began to happen without my being consciously aware of it. I began to become depressed. In fact, I became very pathologically depressed.

By the end of the 1983-84 school year, I was in such bad shape that I couldn't concentrate on the graduate course I was taking at the university where I was working on my master's degree in educational administration (mid-management).

Due to my inability to concentrate and study, I failed my final exam in the course I was taking and ended up making a B, after I had had a strong A going into the exam. I had made 19 A's and only 3 B's in my last 22 college courses.

I became so depressed and disillusioned that I stopped going to graduate school and *never* went back. I had accumulated 27 of the required 36 hours toward my master's degree; I lacked only three courses.

By not returning to graduate school in the ensuing years, I lost all my graduate hours toward my master's degree. (A university allows only a fixed amount of time--usually five years--to complete the work toward a graduate degree, and my time expired.)

* * *

I was depressed and miserable the entire summer of 1984. Marsha's sister Cindy, her husband, and two children came to visit for a week that summer. We all stayed in a luxurious condominium on the beach-front of South Padre Island. I was disconsolate the whole time. Everything I did seemed to take ten times the effort that it should normally require.

I didn't enjoy fishing, eating out, playing games, or swimming. I didn't enjoy anything.

My brother-in-law asked me to help him for a few hours with some maintenance work on his 46-foot gulf boat. I obliged, but the whole time I wouldn't carry on any conversation with him because I was so preoccupied. All I could think about was how horrible my next year of teaching at Memorial was going to be!

Maybe mine was the so-called self-fulfilling prophecy, as psychologists label it, that predestined me to start a bad year that next September.

My depression and anxiety were major contributors; plus there were some less-than-ideal students in my eighth period. My teaching efforts that next school year were doomed.

The 1984-85 school year in Harlingen not only started badly for me, but it also rapidly became worse.

I told my principal that I was contemplating resignation. When he asked me why, all I would admit was that I had an eighth-period class that didn't care anything about learning.

That eighth grade class contained about six incorrigibles between 15 and 18 years old, who were constantly giving me a hard time. The principal said he would transfer the worst three into another class to help me, and he kept his word.

However, for the next three weeks I was still extremely agitated and depressed. I came home on November 2 and told Marsha that I couldn't continue, that I was going to break my contract and resign.

My principal, Lisandro Ramon, was very understanding and considerate. He came to our house to ask if he could be of any other assistance. I declined. The following week I turned in my resignation.

Later, Mr. Ramon would give me a recommendation that would help change my life!

* * *

I decided to begin seeing a psychiatrist again, and I started going to Dr. Robert Collier for help. I was still taking Thorazine and Tofranil. These medications helped me to some degree.

The first thing Dr. Collier wanted to do was to take me off these drugs and put me on Trilafon and Elavil. I was hesitant. Thorazine and Tofranil had helped me conquer my most severe obsession ever. But Dr. Collier was patiently insistent.

I began taking the new medications, and I gradually began to improve.

I firmly believed that I would *never* teach again, that trying to teach *bad* kids had brought on my depression. Dr. Collier disagreed. He insisted that I would have become depressed if I had been a doctor, lawyer, or ditch-digger, that my depression was not brought about because I was a teacher.

I didn't buy this theory at first. For months I kept contending that I would *never* teach again. I looked for a different kind of job in the ensuing months, but I was unsuccessful at finding one.

I had taught for over eight years. Teaching had become such an interwoven part of my life that, I think at least subconsciously, I felt teaching was "my calling."

I really did not want to begin a different career, and this hurt my motivation to put much effort into seeking another type of job.

But at the same time I consciously believed that I could NEVER become a successful teacher.

Not having a job can be most unpleasant. One night, after being out of work for several months, I had an unusual dream. I dreamed that I was working again. I was employed at Memorial Junior High, but not as a teacher. I was working as a janitor, and I was cleaning the boys' restroom. In my dream I seemed to be reasonably happy with what I was doing.

Waking the next morning, I remembered my dream. Then I realized that I wasn't employed, that I was still out of work. A strong feeling of disappointment settled over me. I felt frustrated that the experience had been *only* a dream and that I was still unemployed.

The dream and my reaction to it indicated how downhearted I was about being out of work.

After eight months of not working, I received a call from Jimmy Crow, the superintendent of the small school district at San Perlita. He offered me a job. He and I had become acquainted and had become friends at the Mercedes Livestock Show when we were in high school.

Marsha was beginning to become impatient with my sitting around the house. She and my mother attempted to persuade me to accept the teaching job at San Perlita. I resisted. I believed that I could *never* become a successful teacher. The bad experiences in Laredo and Harlingen had left deep emotional scars.

However, I finally relented and drove to San Perlita to talk to Jimmy Crow. He offered me a job and said that, if I accepted, I would be teaching five different preparations: biology, chemistry, physics, and physical science in high school, plus eighth-grade earth science.

I was very appreciative to Jimmy for offering me employment, but I was also horrified over the *five* preparations! I had never taught more than two courses at once in my career. I thanked Jimmy and said that I would think it over.

I drove away with Marsha, telling her that there was no possibility that I would accept that job. However, I did feel good about being offered steady employment.

We drove directly to my parents' house. My mother came out to the car and asked if I had accepted the job. I told her that I couldn't teach five courses at once.

She became a little angry and said, "This doesn't sound like you, Reagan, and you really need a job!"

We ended our discussion, and Marsha and I drove away. I could sense that Marsha was also upset with me.

Suddenly I remembered that a friend with whom I had taught in Harlingen had called a couple of months previously. He had told me that a science teacher was needed in the Lyford School District, a small district not far from where I lived.

I hadn't acted upon this information because I had really believed that I could never become a successful teacher. But now I told Marsha that I was going to drive to Lyford at that very moment and apply for that job.

This was a decision that changed our lives! However, all was not smooth initially.

Randy Gritzner, the teacher with whom I had worked at Memorial Junior High, knew I was out of work. He had performed an unselfish act by calling me and informing me of the Lyford teaching job. He had told me that the opening was for a sixth-grade science teacher.

When Marsha and I arrived in Lyford, I drove up to the Administration Building and spoke to Leonel Galaviz, Lyford High School principal. I told him that I was interested in applying for the sixth-grade-science teaching position. I asked if he could direct me as to the right building.

I had begun to believe that maybe I could be successful at teaching younger children, and I did have an elementary teaching certificate, which in Texas allows one to teach kindergarten through eighth grade.

Mr. Galaviz told me that the elementary teaching position had been filled. He asked if I would consider teaching in high school. He said an opening existed for a science teacher to teach Biology I, Biology II, and physical science. He asked if I thought I could handle those three preparations.

I replied, "Yes, I can."

I lied. I didn't think for *one moment* that I could be successful filling that position.

Mr. Galaviz asked me why I had left Harlingen, and I told him that I had broken my contract and resigned due to stress brought on by unruly students.

He stated, "Well, it's a strike against you that you broke your teaching contract in Harlingen. Six people have already applied for this position, but not one of them has a teaching certificate as you do. I have just hired a

Harlingen teacher named Randy Gritzner who said he also left Harlingen Memorial because of discipline problems.

"I'll tell you what, Reagan," he continued, "I'll call your principal in Harlingen and ask if he'll recommend you, and I'll also talk to Randy Gritzner about you. I'll then make my determination. I'll let you know by telephone if I can use you."

Marsha and I drove back to Harlingen and said nothing to each other the entire trip. For the rest of that afternoon I was distressed.

What if the phone rang and the Lyford School District offered me that high school teaching job? I didn't want to set myself up to fail a third time at teaching!

The phone rang. I didn't want to answer it. It might be Lyford offering me that job. Then I would have two unpleasant tasks: turning down the job and facing Marsha (who had been supporting us financially for the last six months).

I picked up the phone. It was Lyford. The lady on the line said in a very pleasant tone, "Mr. Smith, come to Lyford and sign your teaching contract. You've been hired."

My heart sank. I should have been exhilarated at this news; instead I was miserable. I managed to stammer, "Thank you," and I hung up the phone.

I told Marsha later that afternoon that I had been offered a contract by Lyford to teach at the high school. Marsha seemed happy, but hers was a *guarded* happiness because she realized I wasn't pleased. I really didn't relish the thought of making a third attempt at teaching!

The next several days I simply went through the motions of doing what I thought to be the *right things*.

I finally forced myself to drive to Lyford and sign my new contract. While I was there, I went to the high school where Mr. Galaviz gave me the textbooks that I would be using. He also told me, "Reagan, I'm taking a chance in hiring you. Please don't make me look bad in the eyes of the superintendent and school board."

I mechanically said that I wouldn't, thanked him, and departed.

I drove home and read through the books. The Biology II textbook was especially thick. I hadn't taken a college biology course in 15 years, and much had changed in the field.

When I was in college only two kingdoms of living organisms were recognized--plants and animals. This text listed five kingdoms, not only plants and animals, but also *monerans*, *protists*, and *fungi*. I hadn't the foggiest notion of what a *moneran* was. This term hadn't been in existence when I was in college. While teaching life science in junior high, I hadn't delved deeply enough into the subject of biology to study terms such as these.

I continued looking through the Biology II text and found multitudes of terms and concepts that I had never heard of. This was getting scary. I began to look through the Biology I book. I found the same thing. That book also contained great numbers of terms with which I wasn't familiar.

I then opened the physical science book. Physical science is related to physics; I had taken three physics courses in college and had made one A and two B's, but that had been eons ago. I felt I had forgotten as much about the subject as I had ever learned.

I became filled with trepidation! In my mind, I *knew* that I could not teach these three courses which I had never taught before! Also, I would now be expected to discipline high school students! I had already had great difficulties making junior high kids behave--I felt sure high school students would be even harder to manage.

The following day as Marsha and I drove through Harlingen, I told her, "Marsha, I just can't accept that Lyford High School teaching position. I should tell Mr. Galaviz soon so he will have time to hire someone else."

Marsha seemed surprisingly understanding. She commented, "I'll bet you feel good, however, just knowing you are presently under contract and gainfully employed."

I had to admit that, yes, it did feel good that I now held a job. I let that thought flow through my mind for a few moments, and I did feel comforted. However, for the next several days, I *truly* believed I would resign from the Lyford teaching position before I ever really began it.

From time to time, though, the haunting words of Mr. Galaviz would invade my consciousness: "Reagan, don't let me down and make me look bad..."

I decided to give my friend Randy a call. Over the phone I told Randy how unsure I was of myself concerning this new teaching job.

Randy is a positive thinker. He said, "Sure you can handle the job, Reagan, and I'll be right next door if you need help."

These words were reassuring. I knew Randy was a Christian. The idea began to trickle through my mind that maybe, just maybe, between Marsha, Randy, the Lord, and myself, I could give the Lyford job a fighting chance.

School was scheduled to begin September 1, and that gave me many more days to contemplate my final decision. I took just one day at a time, as I had learned in AA.

As September 1 approached, I began to feel pressure within me NOT to resign from the job. I didn't want to leave the school district in the predicament of still needing a high school science teacher.

Finally September arrived, and I started back to school. I vividly remember my first day back in the classroom in front of all those high school students. I sweated buckets of perspiration. I'll bet some of the students thought their new science teacher was suffering from malaria!

I survived that first day! The day really went very well. Then I made it through the second day, and the third. Before long I felt in the groove and started enjoying teaching.

Fourteen years have passed since then, and I've enjoyed teaching ever since!

If it had not been for Randy's help, I wouldn't have made it so smoothly through that first year in Lyford.

Randy was also teaching physical science, and he wrote the lessons for that course and shared them with me. This relieved me of enormous pressure and let me concentrate on planning lessons for and teaching Biology I and II.

Something else helped. My principal, Mr. Galaviz, assigned me a teacher's aide the second semester of that first year.

At first I had encountered difficulty in having three new preparations, especially since I was admittedly very deficient in good, quality teaching skills.

I have since learned how to be an effective teacher through study, professional training, and practice. I have also received help from some fellow educators, particularly my dear friends Nancy Trapp and Ouida Yeats, who have been close when I need assistance.

EPILOGUE

I have now been teaching at Lyford High School for fourteen years. I teach anatomy and physiology, environmental science, Biology AP, and Biology I. I have also taught introduction to biology and physical science.

I love my job, and I have felt this way for all the years I have taught in Lyford.

The past fourteen years of my life have undoubtedly been the happiest and most fulfilling years I have ever experienced. The sailing hasn't always been smooth, but the pluses have outweighed the minuses by a healthy margin!

Many of my students tell me how much they enjoy my class and say that they can see my enthusiasm for teaching.

I have had a minimal number of discipline problems as a teacher in Lyford. When students enjoy one's class, discipline usually takes care of itself.

I reached level three of the Texas Teacher Career Ladder (the highest level that was implemented), based upon my good evaluations by my supervisors and the graduate courses I took in college while working on my master's degree.

I have served on the Lyford High School Input Committee, the Administrative Council, and the Site-Based Decision Making Committee. I have sponsored a chess club for students at the high school.

For several years I have served as an usher of the early worship service at the First United Methodist Church in Harlingen, where I am an active member. I have also served on the Worship Committee of that church.

I enjoy playing golf, fishing, swimming, going to movies, eating out, playing chess, reading, working at my computer, traveling, photography, and numerous other activities. The days don't seem to have enough hours for me to do all the things I want to do, and I am enjoying life to its fullest!

Dr. Collier has given me tremendous help during these fourteen years. The medicines he has prescribed for me have made me close enough to normal that I now enjoy living.

* * *

I want to thank Randy Gritzner, whose unselfish phone call one morning led to my getting back into the teaching profession.

I owe many thanks to Lisandro Ramon, my principal at Memorial in Harlingen and later, ironically, my principal in Lyford for a few years. His favorable recommendation to Leonel Galaviz started me off on a third, and finally successful, teaching career.

I am also grateful to Leonel Galaviz for taking a chance on me and hiring me to the Lyford position.

My wife Marsha has now been a registered nurse for twenty-one years. She has stood faithfully by my side in sickness and in health for 30 years, and her unfailing support has sustained me in the roughest times. Marsha is not merely my beloved wife. She is also my best friend!

Dr. Collier has told me that my emotional problems stem from a chemical imbalance in my brain. One of the principal keys to my recovery from mental illness has been medicines that help correct this imbalance and, in so doing, reduce my anxiety.

Valium helped me in the early going. Thorazine and Tofranil did me a world of good by helping me out of the most intense obsession I ever experienced.

The medicines that have led to the last fourteen years' being the most anxiety and OCD free and the happiest are the ones I take now, Trilafon and Elavil. These drugs have worked a miracle in my life. I am grateful to Dr. Collier for finding the medicines which work best for me. I am also thankful for the scientists and pharmaceutical companies who have developed these medicines.

I thank the Good Lord for making possible all these events that have led to the regaining of my *sanity*. I prayed hard for *sanity* for many years, and now it has been granted. My life has been given back to me!

I will probably never be totally OCD free, but the OCD is now much less intense and no longer promotes concern, anxiety, or unhappiness in me. I no longer fear OCD, and this lack of fear has also promoted healing.

I want to stress to any victim of these types of mental illnesses--particularly the anxiety-based disorders such as OCD, phobias, and panic attacks--there is help available if one will just seek it out.

OCD has been called the *secret illness* because many sufferers keep their affliction hidden due to humiliation, embarrassment, and the fear of being labeled *crazy*. I kept my illness a secret from everyone for 20 years.

Today, with the abundance of miracle drugs, there is no need to remain secretive!

Mental illness no longer carries the horrible stigma that it once did. In the past several years many noted people have come forward to admit that they suffer from one or more types of mental ailment.

Mental illness almost ruined my life. However, I am currently a husband, the father of four wonderful children, a successful teacher, a devout Christian, and a well-adjusted, contented, and enthusiastic individual.

I strongly believe that ANY person suffering the torment of anxiety-based disorders can, as I have, become a whole individual again!

* * *

* * *

Any OCD sufferer can find help by contacting the Obsessive-Compulsive Foundation. This foundation is a patient-support organization.

The national headquarter's address for sending correspondence is

Obsessive-Compulsive Foundation
P.O. Box 9573
New Haven, CT 06535
Phone: (203) 315-2190.

This organization publishes a newsletter which can keep the sufferer informed of advances being made. The Obsessive-Compulsive Foundation can also refer him/her to a specialist or a self-help group. Professionally assisted support groups are being formed all over the United States.

APPENDIX

"...For the six million Americans crippled by one or more obsessive-compulsive disorders (OCDs), repetitive, ritualistic behavior like these can be too powerful to control. In fact, left untreated, an OCD can over-run virtually every aspect of a sufferer's life..."
Levenkron, Steven. *Obsessive-Compulsive Disorders.* New York: Warner Books, Inc., 1992.

"...People with OCD may hurt themselves, but NEVER others..." Reported by John J. O'Hearne, M.D.
Vaughan, Joe H. *Alone in the Crowd.* Kansas: Joe Vaughan Associates Communications Services and Publishing, 1993.

"...OCD is now recognized as a common psychiatric disorder in the United States. The lifetime prevalence of 2% to 3% found in the U.S. has also been found in epidemiological studies in several other countries of diverse cultures...Depression and other anxiety disorders frequently co-occur with OCD, which may contribute to misdiagnosis..."
Rasmussen, A.D., J.L. Eisen, Department of Psychiatry and Human Behavior, Brown University. *Journal of Clinical Psychiatry,* 1991.

"...Childhood OCD has been recognized as being more common than previously believed..."
Rapoport, J.L., S.E. Swedo, H.L. Leonard. *Journal of Clinical Psychiatry,* April 1991.

"…it has been estimated that there are at least 20 million individuals in the United States who suffer from one of the many variants of neurotic disorder."
Coleman, James C. *Abnormal Psychology and Modern Life*. Seventh Edition. Glenview, Illinois: Scott, Foresman and Company, 1984.

"...Prominent people throughout history are believed to have suffered from OCD, the 'secret illness'. The famous include John Bunyan, English novelist who penned *The Pilgrims Progress*; Samuel Johnson, another major English writer; and religious reformer Martin Luther. A more contemporary figure, the late billionaire Howard Hughes, was an OCD victim..."
Vaughan, Joe H. *Alone in the Crowd.* Kansas: Joe Vaughan Associates Communications Services and Publishing, 1993.

"...The current eating disorder picture appears to be a modern form of obsessive-compulsive illness beginning during the adolescent period..."
Rothenberg, A., Harvard Medical School. *Psychiatric Clinics of North America,* September 1990.

"...Autistic children are frequently reported to show obsessions and compulsions..."
Baron, Cohen S., University of London. *British Journal of Clinical Psychology,* September 1989.

"...An association between recurrent motor and phonic tics and OCD behaviors has been noted since Tourette's Syndrome was first described. OCD until recently was considered a rare disorder with poor prognosis. Currently, OCD is considered among the most common psychiatric diagnoses...Recent studies suggest a high rate of OCD symptoms in Tourette's Syndrome patients..."
Hollander, E., M.R. Liebowitz, C..M. DeCaria. *Psychiatric Developments,* Winter 1989.

"Anxiety. Whether it manifests itself in panic attacks, phobias, or chronic worry, it's the number-one mental health disorder in America today. But for the twenty to thirty million people whose lives are being disrupted and destroyed by crippling fear, there is new hope..."
Goldman, Mark S., M.D. *The Good News About Panic, Anxiety, and Phobias*. New York: Random House, Inc., 1989.